PHASES OF LIFE WHERE THE GALAX GROWS

BY

MARY NELSON CARTER

FEATURING ORIGINAL PHOTOS BY THE AUTHOR.

infonouveau™
©2012

PHASES OF LIFE WHERE THE GALAX GROWS
Copyright © 2012 Perry Vayo
ISBN: 978-0-6156-5589-5
Published: May 1, 2012
Publisher: Infonouveau™

All rights reserved. No part of this publication may be reproduced, stored in retrieval system, copied in any form or by any means, electronic, mechanical, photocopying, recording or otherwise transmitted without written permission from the publisher. You must not circulate this book in any format.

Original photography by Mary Nelson Carter used for the chapter title pages is presented courtesy of **Special Collections, Appalachian State University**.

Find out more about Infonouveau™ and upcoming books online at
www.infonouveau.com

Printed in the U.S.A.

DEDICATED

To the memory of one who, as friend and physician,
went in and out for years among those
who dwell where the Galax grows.

CONTENTS

Dedication iii
Foreword 1
Chapter 1   Mrs. Smith 6
Chapter 2   Stepping Backwards 23
Chapter 3   A Foggy Day 33
Chapter 4   Mr. Timmins 42
Chapter 5   Playing With Fire 46
Chapter 6   Neighborly Gossip 53
Chapter 7   Barter 60
Chapter 8   The Course of True Love 69
Chapter 9   Hiding Out 78
Chapter 10 In Maria's Garden 85
Chapter 11 The Summer Is Ended 93
Chapter 12 A White Day 100
Chapter 13 Now Is The Winter Of Our Discontent 113
Chapter 14 Sally 120
Chapter 15 Old Times 128
Chapter 16 Getting An Education 138
Chapter 17 Like Other Children 172

About the Author 181
Contact Information 183

Foreword

This book was originally published in 1900 as "North Carolina Sketches, *Phases of Life Where the Galax Grows*", as part of a three volume set of "sketches" about the South. They were set in Tennessee, Georgia, and this one, written by Mary Nelson Carter, set in North Carolina.

Part oral history, part romance novel, part social commentary, *Phases of Life Where the Galax Grows*, is an engaging and enlightening collection of first-person recollections of the daily lives of the people living amongst the hills and hollows near the author's home in Blowing Rock, North Carolina. Describing life in that area, from the Civil War to the end of the century, it is a unique historical record of the personal toll of the war on the people back home, and a window into the culture of Appalachia. An old advertisement for the original series describes them this way:

"Capital Short Stories of the South By Clever Southern Writers

The sketches contained in these volumes seem to be written by the people who are written about. The characteristics and the dialect of the section are treated in natural and convincing fashion, and the stories are all full of human interest. They are indeed exceptionally entertaining contributions to the knowledge of local traits."

Mary Nelson Carter was not always a "southern writer" as advertised by the book's original publisher. She was a Northerner from a family of New England Yankees. The daughter of a well-heeled merchant captain, the family lived in Fairfield, Connecticut. Later, she relocated with her husband to the Philadelphia area, and it was from there that their life-long love of the mountains of North Carolina began. After making several extended trips to that area, they fell in love with the people and the culture of the mountains. Finally, they decided that her husband's skills as a physician were needed by the folks of Blowing Rock, more than by the people of Philadelphia, so, Blowing Rock became their new home.

As a well-educated Northerner, from an affluent family, the cultural gap between the author and the people who populate the book is sometimes evident. No matter how deep her attachment to the place, at times the feeling that Carter is living among the people, without ever being of the people is not hard to pick up. This tension helps the book by injecting some intellectual detachment, allowing for just a bit of social "stick poking" on her part. Whether the "sketch" is an emotional tale of young love and loss in the mountains, or, a compelling retelling of a first-person account of the Civil War years, the reader comes away with a richer understanding of the fabric of the place and time. In that light, *Phases of Life Where the Galax Grows* represents valuable American history and cultural anthropology, by a writer who obviously loves her adoptive home. Whatever its merits or excesses, the book is an entertaining and emotional look at a significant American folk culture, during a time of great change. Sadly, that culture has mostly disappeared today.

My own connection to *Phases of Life Where the Galax Grows* – and the genesis of this project – is a family one. I grew up seeing old dusty copies of "Great, Great, Grandmother Mary's" book up on the shelf in my mother's office. But, it was not until much later that I actually took the time to read one of them. On a whim, I had searched for the book title online, and was amazed to find it in print – in a manner of speaking. An old, ragged copy had been scanned and posted by The Google Books Project, so I ordered a print copy to read – wanting to spare the old volumes anymore wear than needed. When the new volume arrived, I was stunned by the terrible quality of it. Between the missing pages and other pages completely out of order, the book was a mess, and an insult to my ancestor's efforts. My sense of family pride, and the fact that I was already working on another eBook project, that was proving much more complex than expected, led me to decide that resurrecting Mary Carter's book, and getting it back out into the world with the dignity it deserved, was a great reason to take a break from my original project. So, after transcribing the book manually from an original edition, correcting a multitude of typographical errors ignored by the original publisher, sprucing up the layout for the eBook format, and spending far more time on it than planned, *Phases of Life Where the Galax Grows* is ready for a new beginning, in a new century, in a completely new medium.

Read it with an open and willing mind, and enjoy it. But, don't be surprised to come away from it thinking that things don't really change all that much, after all.

– Perry Vayo, Infonouveau, 2012

*"Where Galax grows,
A magic spell
Spreads like a net
O'er hill and dell."*

Mrs. Smith

I

Mrs. Smith, her "old man," and their six grandchildren lived in a two-roomed cabin on a hillside.

There was a good view of the mountains from the hilltop, and when I walked out that way I often stopped in to rest and chat with Mrs. Smith.

She and Bijah had just been married when the war broke out, she told me, and she had many entertaining stories to tell of war times.

"Me and Bijah was livin' down to Coon Branch them times," she said. "Bijah were always mighty peaceable, and he allowed he hadn't no call to go to war. We-uns never did know what it were about, nohow. When the recruitin' officers come round, I done told 'em how Bijah were too puny to chop wood or work much in the craps, and they reckoned he weren't no 'count for a soldier. It's curious how many men's weakly about work," added Mrs. Smith, with a sly twinkle in her eyes; "especially if their women folks is right peart to do it their-selves.

Them were skeery times, and we drawed the bolt on the door nights. One night there come a little knock on the door, and Bijah crept out of bed, and whispered through the crack, 'Who's there?' He daresn't open the door. 'It's me, Bill Sines,' come a voice back. Bill were a free nigger that lived in the holler. 'What you want, Bill?' says Bijah. 'Lemme in, Mr. Smith, fer God's sake! and I'll tell you,' Bill says. So Bijah opened the door a crack, and Bill slipped in, and shut it quick, scared-like. He says in a whisper: 'It's four Union soldiers, escapin' from prison. There's six of 'em, but two's give out, and they done hid 'em in the woods. T'others is nigh perished. I done told 'em you-uns know the road to Bentonville better'n most, and I allowed mebbe you'd come a piece of the way with us, Mr. Smith.' Bill knowed Bijah were right soft-hearted, and hated it bad to see a body sufferin'.

'I ain't never been fur on that road myself,' says Bill; 'and them poor fellows is like to be ketched if they lose their way. They'se waitin' whilst I come in to ax you,' Bill says.

I done told him to fetch 'em in. My Lor', they was a sight! I never see the beat. I expect they hadn't lived like they was the top of the heap in prison, and they'd been dodgin' in the woods for more'n a week, and was nigh starved. We-uns give 'em every bite there were in the house. Victuals weren't none to plenty them times," she added, with a grim smile. "It were little enough, but they daresn't wait for me to cook nothin', or I'd have made 'em some bread. I were that sorry for 'em I could have cried. They was mighty polite and obleeged fer what we-uns done for 'em. They asked would we watch out for t'other two, and we said we would.

Bijah took his ax, like he were goin' to chop, and a bag o' corn, like we were goin' to mill, for the mill were on the way, and sot out with Bill to show 'em the road. Bill he had his gun, like he were 'possum huntin'.' He done told the soldiers that the neighbors knowed as niggers was powerful fond o' 'possums. They smiled kind-like at him, but a body could see how they was a-studyin' and wasn't pay'n no heed to Bill's foolishness. Bijah said none of 'em spoke nary a word after they got out of doors, and it were sort of creepy-like in the dark. The night were plum black and foggy, and Bijah said he kept a-seein' bears and men jumpin' for 'em at every turn, but he kept right on, and never told t'others. He were plum glad he brung his ax – but, Lor' me! Bijah's that soft-hearted he can't hardly kill a chicken. I don't reckon he'd have got much good out of his ax if anybody'd got after 'em.

As luck would have it, nobody met up with 'em, and him and Bill had sot the prisoners well on their way before sun-up. Then they come along back by way of the mill, to get the corn ground. Mr. Hanscum, the miller, was takin' on powerful that mornin'.

'You-uns ain't seen no rascally Yanks as you come along, has ye?' he says, first thing.

'How many was there?' says Bijah, simple like.

'Six on 'em, escapin' from prison,' says the miller. 'The home guards is after 'em, and I hope they'll hang every one of 'em.'

'Mebbe them's 'em we see, Bill,' says Bijah, nudgin' Bill to make him quit lookin' scared.

'Where at?' says Bill, catchin' on. 'Them men down in the holler? There were a heap more'n six o' them. I'se skeered when I see 'em, and so's you, old man. We didn't wait to ax 'em their names,' Bill says, laughin' out loud.

'Where be they at?' says the miller, stoppin' the mill, with Bijah's corn in the hopper, and catchin' up his gun.

'Over yonder,' says Bijah, pointin' jest contrary to where the men was gone. 'But ain't you goin' to grind my corn, Mr. Hanscum?'

'No sir! I'd a sight rather hunt Yanks.'

Bijah let on like he were mighty mad, and allowed as he'd have to go to some mill that were 'tended to right; but the miller quit, without waitin' to hear what he were sayin'. I ain't never heard whether them four prisoners got clear; but we reckoned they did, 'cause we'd have likely heard if they'd been took. But the home guards come up with the two poor sick ones, and shot 'em. Bill said he done heard 'em tell t'others, when they parted from 'em, that they wouldn't never be took alive, so we allowed they'd fit back at the home guards. We-uns hated it bad, but we had to keep our mouths shut war times, for fear o' gettin' shot ourselves. There wouldn't never be no war if I had my way. What gets me is to see them that was fit to tear one another to pieces them days, right good friends now. Accordin' to my notion, folks has a sight to learn before the millennium catches 'em," Mrs. Smith finished with a laugh.

II

"There were a right smart o' raidin' 'long towards the last o' the war," says Mrs. Smith one day, "and one side were as bad as t'other. It didn't make no difference which side you was on; if you had anythin', they took it. Old Mis' Gaston were about the only one I heard tell of that got ahead of 'em. Her and her folks kept a public, and they done there own stillin', so they had a sight o' whiskey laid by. They had right smart o' stock, too. They was mighty forehanded. Somehow they got word, after one of the big battles, that the mountings was plum full o' raiders and stragglers. So they all sot to work to hide what they had. Old Mis' Gaston were like a man for boss'n things. She first sot the least boys to takin' out a lot o' stones from under the side of the house, where it were walled up. There weren't no cellar. Then she sot the big boys and gals to makin' fires and hangin' big pots of water over 'em, while she and her old man sharpened up the knives and the ax. There hogs and chickens was all penned up, against a time like this; so there weren't no time lost catchin' 'em. The old man and the biggest boy done killed 'em, to the last one, and while Mis' Gaston and the gals was cleanin' and scaldin' 'em, and burnin' up the leavin's, so they wouldn't tell tales, the rest was puttin' the kegs of whiskey under the house.

But Mis' Gaston were bossin' the whole job. She says to the boys: 'Leave one full barrel and one that's nigh used up on the porch, and put some empty kegs there, too. They'll think we done hid 'em if they don't find nary one. Now throw that old cloth over 'em, like we was tryin' to hide 'em.'

Chapter 1: Mrs. Smith

They done just like she said, and then they all went to work to hide the hog meat and chickens and other victuals. Mis' Gaston made 'em leave some scrap pieces of smoked meat in the smokehouse, and a big cut o' cheese layin' in the pantry. She wouldn't let 'em hide all the corn, neither, for fear o' makin' the soldiers too suspicious. When everything were safe under the house, she stood by 'til the stones was all laid up like they was before. Nobody'd a knowed they'd been took out.

After everything about the house were done, she says to the boys to drive the two cows up into the steepest and rockiest place they could find in the woods. She give 'em a pan o' salt to take along to put on the rocks for 'em to lick, and a bag o' corn for 'em to eat their fill, hopin' they'd lay down and chew their cuds and not come home. The gals done milked 'em dry before they went. They throwed out all the folks couldn't drink of the milk, so nobody'd know they had any cows.

Mis' Gaston were plum tired after everything were done, and she sot down on the porch to rest a bit. She said she never see a prettier day. 'Peared like there couldn't be no war. The sky were so blue, that the trees were standin' up agin' it like they was painted in a pictur. She was thinkin' to herself that no pictur couldn't be half so pretty, when she heard such a noise down the road that she know'd the soldiers was comin'. She and the gals let on to be sewin', and the old man and the boys was workin in the garden. Up come a lot of Yankee soldiers, cussin' and swearin' like they'd been drinkin'. Mis' Gaston asked what did they want. They talked back mighty rough, and threatened to shoot 'em all if they didn't fetch out what whiskey they had.

Mis' Gaston showed 'em the kegs that was under the cloth, and said they were all she had. She let on like she were cryin', and said couldn't they leave 'em a little for sickness? They didn't pay no heed to what she were sayin', but went for the whiskey. It made 'em so rough actin' that she were gettin' right scared, and had just told the

11

gals they must slip out and hide, when up gallops a officer on horseback. When the men see him they sobered up mighty quick, and slunk out into the road. He jawed 'em awful for gettin' drunk, and they followed him like they was whipped dogs.

They hadn't touched nothin' but the whiskey, and Mis' Gaston and her folks was laughin' how easy they'd got off. They reckoned they'd fry some o' the chickens for supper and maybe fresh hog meat too. While they's talkin' about it, up comes about twenty Confederates. They says first thing, 'Got any whiskey?' 'I could have give you some,' says Mis' Gaston, 'if them blamed Yankees hadn't stole it all not two hours ago.'

'Phew!', says the orderly, 'be they so nigh as that? We'd better light out o' this mighty quick, boys. Give us what you got to eat, ma'am, and we'll go 'long.'

'It's mighty little,' says Mis' Gaston, kind of doleful, 'Them Yankees was for grabbin' everythin' we had. If it hadn't been for their Capting comin' along and jawin' 'em for gettin' drunk, we-uns might go hungry. Poor folks has a mighty poor chance these days', she says, burstin' into tears.

'Well', says the man, 'we-uns has got to eat, too; but we'll leave you a snack.'

So, they looked round and carried off nigh all there were. They was in a hurry, 'count o' the Yankees bein' so nigh. They hadn't had no liquor on the way, 'cause the Yankees was ahead of 'em; so they was more politer.

After it got plum dark, Mis' Gaston allowed that it were safe for 'em to get some supper. Exceptin' for the milk some on 'em drunk, they hadn't took time to eat a bite all day. They was that hungry, they didn't waste no time pickin' the chicken bones, and they was that tired that old Mis' Gaston allowed they wouldn't have knowed what killed 'em if the soldiers had come back and murdered 'em all in their beds. They was mighty proud they done saved their things though," Mrs. Smith concluded.

III

Mrs. Smith had an eye for the beauties of nature, and I found her one warm June day sitting on a rock on the hilltop enjoying the view. "My Lor', but it's warm," she said, fanning herself with her sunbonnet. "I get het up workin' in the corn patch. Ain't it pretty up here? I often come up here to rest and get away from the children. They'se mighty pesterin' some days.

Look at that big fire off towards Hawk's Bill. It 'minds me of war times. When we see a big fire 'way off, we was 'feared it were the enemy sot it, or mebbe a big battle goin' on. Them were oneasy times.

If you like to hear war stories so well, I must tell you about Mr. Boner's folks. They lived about two miles from Mis' Gaston. They didn't get off so well as she done, though. Mr. Boner were right well-to-do, and he had a sight o' hog meat hanging in his smokehouse. He'd done killed all his hogs for winter. He had a big crap of corn and rye that year, too. The Confederates was the first to come by his house the day he were raided. He see 'em goin' for the smokehouse, and he hollers out for 'em to take the key and open the door right. 'There ain't no need o' my havin' to buy a new padlock, boys, 'count o' your bein' in a hurry,' he says to 'em. He were so pleasant-spoke that they didn't take all the meat, like they'd meant to, nor all his corn and rye. They see he were a sympathizer.

He locked up the smokehouse after they was gone, and when his folks was worryin' about losin' so much, he reckoned 'tweren't no use cryin' over spilt milk.

Next day here come some Yankees. He give 'em the key the same way. He done told 'em they wasn't right sharp or they'd'a got there ahead o' t'others. They was right civil, but they done cleaned him out.

Old Mis' Boner were most cryin' t'other day when she were tellin' me about the hard times they had scratchin' along that winter. She allowed the soldiers wouldn't have come pesterin' of 'em if Mr. Boner had a' hid away their things like Mis' Gaston done. The old man sot by the fire laughin' while she's talkin'. When she were through, he says, 'Well, I done saved my padlock, Ma.' Then he laughed 'til she had to pat him on the back. When he ketched his breath again, he says to her, 'And you mustn't forget how we done saved Si.' Si's their gal Miry's man," Mrs. Smith explained.

"Old Mis' Boner laughed, too. Then she done told me the whole story about Miry and Si courtin'. I knowed it all before, but I like to hear her talk. So does her old man. A body'd think he'd get tired listenin' to her. He don't seem to, though. He sets by and laughs every time, like he'd never heard her tellin' the same thing before. Mis' Boner says they plum hated the Yankees, and it were all she could do that day to keep from spittin' on 'em. She chaws, and she's always a-spittin'.

The old man's right peaceable, and he done told her to hold her jaw and not go nigh them Yankees, if she knowed when she were well off. She 'lowed he were right, but she says it went agin' her to do like he said.

Miry weren't sixteen then. She were right peart lookin'; her hair were black and curly, and her eyes 'minded you of stars dark nights. Her cheeks was that red you'd most want to eat 'em. I'm sayin' it like the fellers talked about her. Her teeth was better'n common, too, 'count of her not dippin' snuff.

When the Yankees come in, there were one of 'em mighty peaked-lookin'; a right young chap he were. He done sot down on the doorstep and groaned. Miry heard him, and run out to see if he was hurt. She were right good-hearted. When he see her he groaned worser. She said could she do anythin' to help him. Lor', yes; he 'lowed she could, leastwise if she was strong enough to help him off with his heavy knapsack. She reckoned she were. He didn't help her none, so it took time.

He 'peared like he were gettin' worse every minute, and she wished her Ma or somebody'd come. Mis' Boner kept out of the way. She 'lowed she wouldn't touch one of them Yankees with a ten-foot pole; not even if he was dyin'. T'other Yankees was cleaning out the smoke house and corncrib.

Miry axed this one what ailded him. He allowed it were cramp colic. 'Oh, Lord!,' he says, doublin' all up. She know'd hot whiskey and water were good for that, so she run in to get some. Mis' Boner began to jaw her for foolin' with a Yankee.

'Oh shut up, Ma; you ain't got no feelin'. He's half dead,' says Miry, runnin' out again with the liquor.

It were the first time in her life that Miry'd ever sassed her Ma. Mis' Boner nigh about fainted when she heard her. It didn't keep her from peekin' through the crack of the door, though, to see what they was up to.

When the soldier smelled the whiskey, he says: 'Thank you kindly, Miss, but I'm temperance. I wouldn't drink that stuff if I was dyin'.

'Yes, you would, too,' says Miry, right resolute, seizin' him round the neck and pourin' it down his throat like he were a naughty child. It nigh about choked him. Mis' Boner thought he'd never come to. He kept on leanin' up agin' Miry, and lettin' on like he'd never get his breath. Miry were so scared she forgot to take away her arm, and she kept fannin' him with her apron. When he heard t'other Yankees comin', he sot up.

'My pain's gone, Miss,' he says, smilin' at Miry. 'You're the best doctor I ever see; but if I go to the devil with drink, it'll be all along of you.'

He see she were like to cry then, so he laughed, and told her she needn't be scared, for he'd always hated the stuff. He made all kinds of excuses to keep her nigh him, 'til she said she must go now and see if her Ma needed her. Then he let on like the pain were comin' back. It were, too, but not so bad as first-off. He said he wouldn't take no more whiskey, for fear it would make him tight, not bein' used to the stuff. But he allowed if she'd rub his cold hands with her warm ones, that would do him more good.

Mis' Boner kept on peekin', and she says she never seen a gal made sich a fool of; but Miry didn't seem to sense it. Well, the long and the short of it were that when t'others got ready to go, this one were too sick to march, and they had to leave him behind. Mis' Boner were that mad, she says, she could have choked him in earnest. She daresn't say nothin', though, and it ended by her and Miry havin' to nurse him through the fever. First off, Mis' Boner allowed he were playin' 'possum, but Miry know'd better.

He weren't nothin' but a boy, but he were a right likely one. When he were out of his head he never talked nothin' but clean talk that couldn't shame nobody; and he were always calling for his Ma and Pa and the rest of his folks. He'd think Mis' Boner and Miry was some on 'em and beg 'em to kiss him before he died, especially Miry; and she done it to keep him quiet. They reckoned he were goin' to die and it wouldn't matter nohow. He's livin' yet," said Mrs. Smith, smiling.

"Soon as he got so's he could talk straight," she resumed, "he done told 'em all about his folks. They was rich, and he were their only son. He were away at college, and he were plum crazy to go to war, 'long with the neighbor boys, but his Pa wouldn't hear to it. So, he run off and 'listed. He done told 'em he were of age, so they'd take him. He allowed the Lord wouldn't count that kind of a lie agin' him; but I dunno.

His folks took on powerful when they heard it. They wanted to buy him off. It were easy to do that up North, and git some other feller to go in your place. He wouldn't give in to it though. He see mighty hard times, but he wouldn't never complain, and this were the first spell o' sickness he'd had. It were nigh to being the last, too. Mis' Boner allows as he'd'a died sure if it weren't for Miry. She says she never see the like o' the way that girl kept up to wait on him. 'Peared like he couldn't stir, night nor day, but she were right there, fussin' over him like he were a baby. One spell, when he were right weak, he'd cry if he see her go out o' the room.

Before he got so's to sit up, he told Miry he loved her so that unless she agreed to marry him, he couldn't never get well. He were dyin' right then, he told her, and nothin' but thinkin' she'd marry him could keep him alive. He worked on her feelin's, sayin' how hard his folks would take it if he's to die. Miry allowed they'd feel worser if he was to marry a poor girl like her; but he wouldn't hear to that, so she give in.

Mis' Boner says they hated it mighty bad havin' her marry a Yankee. They hadn't nothin' agin' Si himself; they liked him splendid; they plum forgot he were a Yankee, he were so nice. They see Miry were sot on him, and it went agin' 'em to cross her, anyway. Miry were a right good girl.

When he got well enough, he went away off to join his regiment. He writ back to Miry that he done told his folks all about her, and they sent her their love. They allowed it were her what saved his life, and they wouldn't put nothin' in the way of his marryin' her. But they reckoned she'd ought to go to a good school, and get a eddication like him. When the war were over, they sent money for her to go up North to school, nigh to where they lived.

Her and Si was married two years afterwards. Nobody but old Mis' and Mr. Boner calls him Si to his face, though. It's Mr. and Mrs. Appleton when the neighbors talk of Miry and her man. They're a right handsome couple, and they behave handsome to the old folks too. They had 'em up to live with 'em, and treated 'em splendid; but

Mis' Boner says they live too fine for the likes of her and Mr. Boner, and she can't never feel to home up there.

She's got a whole trunkful of fine clothes Miry and Si give 'em, but they never put 'em on. She keeps 'em under the bed. If you ask her, she'll get 'em out to show you; but most times, I reckon, she disremembers she's got 'em. She allows homespun's good enough for her and her old man. But they're right proud of Miry and Si and their bein' so rich and happy. 'Pears like Mis' Boner never gets tired tellin' their story," said Mrs. Smith smiling.

IV

One day in autumn I was sitting on the hill above Mrs. Smith's house, idly watching the rise and spread of smoke from the many fires among the mountains.

The landscape was gorgeous with autumn coloring, and the dying leaves were falling thickly about me.

Having seen nothing of Mrs. Smith as I passed the house, I was startled when she suddenly appeared beside me. She laughed. "I reckon you're afraid o' ghosts, ain't you?" she asked. "Say you ain't? I be. I never see but one, and maybe Ma were right, and it weren't one, nohow. All the same, it give me the sort o' scare you can't never git over. This kind o' day always puts me in mind of it. The air smelt o' smoke, and the leaves was a-rattlin' down on your head everywheres, just like they be now.

It were when Bijah and me was courtin'. I'd been to the settlemint to swap soft soap and tree sugar for store goods, and it were gettin' on towards dark as I come along back. I weren't skeery then, and I weren't in no hurry." She smiled.

"When a girl's got a sweetheart," said she, "she's always kind o' lookin' out for him to catch up with her somewheres on the road. But if she's got any spunk, she don't let him know she's watchin' out for him. That's how it were with me. I heard a kind o' rustlin' in the leaves comin' on behind me, and I allowed it were Bijah. I never turned my head, but kept right on like I didn't hear nothin'.

Pretty soon I begin to feel queer all over, for it 'peared like I were bein' follered on the sly. I knowed Bijah couldn't stand it not to speak all that time. Then I thought I'd better walk faster. Just that minute there were a sort of crash behind me. I give one look back, and see somethin' white movin' in the woods 'longside the road. Then I give a screech, and I never quit runnin' 'til I stumbled on the step and fell in the door at home. I cut my lip and hurt my head bad, and I were that scared I ain't never been easy in my mind since if I'm out after dark. Ma reckoned it were Mis' Bland's old white cow I see, but I knowed better. I made her promise she wouldn't tell, for I hated it to have fun poked at me. But she asked Mis' Bland where were her cow that night, and Mis' Bland said she done wandered off, and didn't come home 'til next evenin'. Ma couldn't never git it out of my head that it were a ghost, though."

"Is that a ghost or a cow?" I asked, pointing to a moving object on the hillside.

"'Tain't neither one," replied Mrs. Smith. "It's one o' them artist fellers paintin' picturs. The mountings is plum full of 'em," she added, "A body'd think they could git some kind o' work to do if they tried. Some on 'em's right biggotty.

Mis' Sand went to one of 'em to git him to paint her pictur, and he said he weren't no photographer. She allowed she knowed that; that were the reason she wanted him to do it for her, so's to put in red cheeks and her blue dress. She done told him so. He allowed his prices was too high for her. She got kind o' mad, and done told him she reckoned she knowed her own business. He said how much were she allowin' to pay. She done told him a dollar. He laughed right out. 'Mis' Sand,' he says, 'I ain't paintin' nary picturs for nobody for less than fifty dollars, and that's cheap.'

I reckon he were pokin' fun at her, but Mis' Sand allows he were in earnest.

When I were young, one o' them artist fellers used to come up here summers. Us gals done a sight o' what he called posin' for him. But, Lor' me, as I done told Ma, I'd a heap ruther work in the corn. A body gits plum tired standin' or sittin' still. Them drawin's he make hadn't no more look o' me than that dog's got. I always let on like I thought they had, though, for it ain't polite to hurt a body's feelin's. He were a mighty kind man hisself.

Makes me think o' war times. Not long after the war bust out, one o' them artist fellers come up into the mountings nigh to where I lived. He were a city chap. He'd had the fever, and were right puny. He couldn't go to the war, nohow, bein' so weakly, and his doctor done told him to stay in the mountings 'til he got strong.

He brung his paint things along for company. His doctor allowed he'd git well a heap quicker if he staid out o' doors all he could. So he'd take his things and paint picturs of the mountings nigh about all day. He done showed 'em to we-uns, as he come along by, but I never see nothin' to 'em.

He were always talkin' agin' the Yankees, and sayin' how he'd fight 'em when he got strong and well. But some o' the home guards got it into their heads as he were a Yankee spy. They reckoned them picturs he were paintin' was to make a map o' the mountings with. I knowed better, for I were acquainted with some o' his kin folks. Besides, couldn't nobody pretend to hate the Yankees like he done. They'd git tripped up sometimes. He didn't. It were always the same kind o' talk and the same sort o' black looks every time. I told some o' the home guards so, but they allowed I'd better be careful myself; so I done shut up.

But I give Mr. Todd – that were his name – a hint. You never see a body so mad. It weren't the Yankees he were goin' to fight now, but the the home guards," she went on, laughing as she spoke.

"'And to think my people belong to the best blood in the Old North State!' he says, most shoutin'; 'and now she's seceded, ain't I bound to stand by her?'

I allowed I didn't know how that were, but I says, 'You're bound to git into trouble if you set the home guard agin' you.' Sure enough, the very next day but one, some on 'em went to his boardin' place while he were out paintin' picturs. They done upset all his things, but they didn't find nothin'. As for his picturs of the mountings, they reckoned as the Yankee weren't livin' that were smart enough to make head or tail out of 'em nohow.

They didn't pester him no more, but you never see a madder feller than he were when he found out what they'd done. His face got as red as them maple leaves. His people's mighty hot-headed.

He allowed as the Yankees couldn't 'a' served him no meaner trick, and he quit talkin' agin' 'em. Poor feller! He didn't live to fight nobody. He done took pneumony fever, and died that very fall."

Mrs. Smith shaded her eyes with her hand while she surveyed our artist neighbor at his work.

"That feller's been settin' over there all the mornin'," she began. "I see him when I come up to hunt the cow. That white thing you see is his umbrell. I reckon he's afraid the sun'll fade him," she added, chuckling. "I asked one o' the boarder ladies t'other day what she done put powder on her face for. She laughed, and said it were to keep her from fadin'," said Mrs. Smith.

Then, pushing back her sunbonnet and wiping her face on her apron, she added; "The sun *is* mighty hot to-day. Hope it won't fade my gownd," added she, laughing heartily at her own joke. "I got a better one, but I keep *it* to wear to preachin' and Sunday-school. I reckon the Lord don't do nothin' to keep his trees and things from fadin'. The way the leaves is droppin' down round you on that there rock is like a red and yaller snowstorm. First big wind comes long'll take nigh all of 'em off the trees. I hate to see 'em fall, but I reckon it's the Lord's way o' keepin' the world a-goin'. I just love to see 'em all puttin' out fresh in the spring. I wonder if it'll be that way with we-uns," said she, wistfully. "'Pears like we're goin' the way o' the leaves and the flowers."

"'We all do fade as a leaf,'" I quoted, lightly. "'As a flower of the field, so he flourisheth.'"

"Yes; ain't it right queer," she rejoined, quickly, "how the Bible's got somethin' in it to fit everything a body does or says? It's a heap o' comfort. Even war times," she continued, "when you didn't hear nothin' but about battles and killin', and 'peared like your eyes was full o' blood whichever way you looked, you kept a-thinkin' o' things the Bible said.

My Pa and my youngest brother was both killed in the same battle. Them was black days. I kept a-sayin' over to myself every comfortin' thing I could remember out o' the Bible. It didn't help Ma much, though. She were plum broke down after the news came. I never see her laugh again. She were like the leaves; she just faded away."

After a short silence, Mrs. Smith said, cheerfully: "Well, them times is past and gone. "'Tain't no kind o' use mournin' about 'em now.

This is a mighty pretty day; everything's so quiet and peaceful. Just listen to them hens cacklin' away down in yonder cove!

Wisht I could set up here awhile longer with you, but there's my old man callin'. 'Yes, I'm a-comin'," she called back to him, with a laugh in her tones. "I can't help laughin'," said she. "'Pears like he can't get along nohow unless I'm somewheres in sight," Mrs. Smith added, as she started down the hill.

Chapter 2
Stepping Backwards

Stepping Backwards

The rhododendrons and azaleas were in bloom, their brilliant hues running riot through the woods and filling the mountains with glory. Like an ignis fatuus, their marvelous coloring, set off by the background of green leaves or blue sky, had led me on until I found myself far from home.

The shadows were lengthening, and I was tired enough to welcome the sight of the open doorway of a cabin, where I was met by a friendly invitation to "Come in, and set awhile," which I accepted.

I had known something of the Simmons family, but this was my first visit to their home. I needed rest and Mrs. Simmons in her turn appeared to find my advent an agreeable break in the day's monotony.

The woods had seemed ablaze with glowing fires, as the flame-colored azaleas leaped into view, and in this homely room the dancing reflections from a bright fire on the hearth lent a strange charm where the sun would have revealed only rugged ugliness. Except for the fire, there was no light but that coming in through the open doorway.

After chatting awhile with Mrs. Simmons, I asked how long her family had been living in that house. From the general air of disorder about the place, I thought they were new tenants.

"Oh, always," she replied. "My Pa and Ma done lived here before me. I done lived along o' them after Timothy and me got married. After Pa died, Ma lived along o' we-uns."

"But you seem to have begun a new house," said I.

"Yes; them old j'ists and rafters *is* just a sight," interrupted Mrs. Simmons. "I tell my old man I wisht he'd burn the hull lot and get shut of 'em. He won't do it, 'cause he 'lows as he'll have a turn of luck some time, and they'll come in handy to build another house with. He didn't never begin it. It were my Pa, before he got so poorly them last three year. He's been dead nigh on twenty year.

The frame were all covered in, and some of the ceilin' were up, too – stripes o' yaller pine and cherry it were. Pa allowed to make it mighty pretty inside. Some of the floorin' were down, and there were a sight o' work done to that house before Pa died."

"Why, there's nothing but a bare frame now!" I exclaimed in astonishment.

"No," said Mrs. Simmons, complacently. "Timothy's always had a powerful hurtin' in his side whenever he done any right hard work, and he reckoned it weren't no kind o' use him tryin' to finish a big job like that. It takes a sight of wood to keep fires going," added Mrs. Simmons, as she stirred up a blaze with the long pole she used for a poker. Thrusting the burning end of it into the ashes to cool, she continued: "Timothy allowed we-uns might as well burn up the stuff in the new house as to leave it for other folks. It were a sight easier'n choppin' out in the woods. I'd ought to know, for I done most of the choppin', 'long o' him being so puny.

Ma done cried first-off when she heard him pullin' the sidin' off the new house; but, Lor' me, women folks ain't got no say about such things; men's mighty masterful. I hated it, too, the worst way, but it were powerful easy to slip out and get wood off the new house when Ma and the young 'uns was cold and Timothy was down to the settlemint. He allows he'll build a better house than that when his luck turns."

I asked what work he did. I had seen him loafing about the village every time I had occasion to go there.

"Oh, he don't do no right *hard* work, nohow, " said Mrs Simmons, " 'count of the crick in his side; but he allows he'll get a nice soft job sometime and make big money. Me and the children does most of the work, and Sabiny and me, that's my biggest gal, does a heap of boarders' wash."

Changing the subject, Mrs. Simmons said: "My Pa's name were Moyer. He come from way up in Pennsylvany. He weren't none of your low-down, no-'count trash, like some on 'em," said she, tossing her head.

"He'd travelled a sight, my Pa had. He drove on a canal boat when he were young, and he done told us a heap about the things he'd saw. But he enjoyed poor health up there, 'long o' the hard winters. He had the phthisic powerful bad. The doctors done told him he'd live a sight longer down here among the mountings. That's how he come to be here.

He could do a heap more work than some as is a sight weller, though. He done took up this here land from the State, and he cleared most of it hisself. Then he put up this house and married my Ma. He stayed 'long o' her folks when he first come. She were a right pretty gal, with red cheeks, then, and it weren't long before they was courtin'. My Ma were a mighty good woman, but she hadn't no eddication. My Pa he had. He could read out o' the Bible like he were preachin', and he took a sight o' trouble tryin' to learn we'uns to read and write. There weren't no school nigh us in them days. Ma always said what were the use pesterin' of us; she done well enough without a eddication. So we growed up same as Ma done. We'd a heap rather be out 'long o' Pa and Ma burnin' brush and such than tryin' to get book learnin'."

"Was the family large?"

"There were only Joshuay and me. He's been dead nigh on thirty year. Just before Pa died, he done told Ma to send to the city and get a pretty white stone for his grave, like his folks up in Pennsylvany always had. He said for her to get her own name writ on it, too, for he reckoned Timothy wouldn't never get no more stones for nobody. Pa didn't always set sich store by Timothy as he'd ought to. Ma done got the stone, but, Lor', when it come home all boxed up, it were that white and pretty she weren't willin' to have it out in the weather; so she done kep' it under her bed 'til she died.

It were mighty onconvenient, for the sweet 'tater cellar is right under that bed. You see Ma slept nighest the fire, 'count of her feelin' the cold, and you're just bound to keep sweet 'taters nigh the fire.

It ain't to say a real cellar; it's just a hole, and loose boards over it. 'Taters needs a sight of airin', and Timothy'd get that vexed havin' that stone to move every time. He sets a sight o'store by sweet 'taters for eatin', though," said Mrs. Simmons, laughing. "Ma allowed if he could eat such a sight of 'em, it wouldn't do him no hurt to move that 'ere stone once in awhile. Him and the boys done sot it up out there by Pa's and Ma's graves after she died.. They's buried out there where you see them cows."

I saw some pigs, too, and asked Mrs. Simmons if they were rooting in the family burial lot.

"Yes," she replied; "no keepin' of 'em out. Pa fixed that lot up mighty fine after Joshuay died. The grave were all flowers, and he had nice green grass growin', and he put up a good tight fence; couldn't even a chicken get in, let alone horgs. Did you say where's it gone? Oh, fences don't last no time. Timothy allowed we-uns might as well burn up the pieces as to let 'em lie there and rot. Horgs don't root deep enough to disturb corpses, nohow, and Timothy reckons the way his peoples buried is good enough for we-uns.

Pa used to talk a sight about his old home, and along to the last he allowed he'd made a dreadful mistake not takin' Ma and goin' back there, so's we-uns could get a eddication. But Ma were always plum sot agin' it. Pa liked her splendid, but he couldn't abide tobacco and snuff, and he said no decent woman wouldn't use 'em where he come from, and Ma'd just have to quit 'em if she went up there. She were always a powerful hand for a chew-stick. She used to give 'em to we-uns when we's little, to keep us still. That's how I took to dippin', and Sabiny same way," said Mrs Simmons, spitting into the fire.

"Ma said couldn't nobody make her see no harm in tobacco. Timothy and the boys chaws. We-uns raises our own tobacco," continued Mrs. Simmons, with evident pride. "We raises a sight, so Timothy has it to swap at the stores sometimes."

I remarked that Timothy seemed to spend a great deal of time at the stores.

"Yes; men folks has to be where there's somethin' goin' on,' especially rainy days, " she replied. "'Tis mighty dull settin' round home all day; nobody can't blame 'em.

Timothy's different from most, too. He's always allowing as he'll hear of a nice soft job o' work up to the settlemint. Some nights when he comes home all done out with such a long walk, and bein' disappointed agin', he says, 'No luck yet, old gal.' Then I chirk up and bid him mind how the preacher says as some is always down on their luck in this world, but it'll be made up to 'em in the next. Now, my Pa weren't no believer in luck, except about sickness; and he 'lowed we'd get shut of a sight of that if we took better care of ourselves."

"Why, you have got a window in your house, Mrs. Simmons," I exclaimed , irrelevantly, as I caught sight of the shuttered opening in the wall. "I have been wondering how a man like your father came to build a house without one."

"Yes; Pa set a heap o' store by plenty of light and air. There's another winder back of you; we-uns ain't so bad off as you allowed."

"So I see," I replied; "but why don't you open the window and let in the light?"

"Well, when Pa built this house, he couldn't get no glass lights; so he put shutters with leather hinges on the windows. We done kept 'em open always in pretty weather. After Pa died the wind blowed 'em loose on their hinges, and they kept Timothy awake windy nights; so he nailed 'em fast, and there they be ever since. He allows he'll put a sight o' glass lights in the new house he's goin' to build when his luck turns."

Mrs. Simmons stooped over the fire, drawing to one side a bed of hot coals, on which to set her bake-oven. While she talked, she had been mixing and rolling out the soda biscuits for the evening meal. Seeing the amount of soda which went into them, I was glad I had a good excuse for declining the kindly invitation she gave me to stay to supper. I was much interested in her primitive facilities for cooking, however. I asked if there were no crane in the fireplace for suspending the pot and pans over the fire.

"Not now there ain't," replied Mrs. Simmons. "Pa put in a good one; he got the blacksmith to make it like what Pa's folks had at home, but it got broke. Timothy ain't no hand to run round gettin' things fixed; so there it lays in the corner."

Even the dancing firelight, as she bent over the hearth, could not soften or glorify the awkward gauntness of a figure like that of Mrs. Simmons. She wore her black hair strained back from a bony, high forehead; her skin was wrinkled and sallow, and her eyes light and watery. The stain of tobacco was about her mouth; her hands were coarse and grimy, and so were the garments she wore.

Rising stiffly after adjusting her bake-oven over the coals, she asked, abruptly; "Ever hear tell of my Sammy? Say you ain't? Pa named him after hisself, and he done sot a heap o' store by him. He learned him his letters when we weren't more'n three year old, and when he were six he could read nigh every kind of print.

Pa were sick more'n three year before he died. He had a kinsumption, and he were powerful bad off 'long to the last. He were always telling Sammy he wanted him to make somethin' of hisself; them's his very words; and when he got big enough, he must go up to Pennsylvany and find Pa's folks and tell 'em who he were. He kep' a-sayin', 'Be sure you git a eddication, Sammy.' It were a sight the way the little feller took on when his grandpop died."

"And did he take his grandfather's advice?"

"'Peared like he done cared more than ever for book learnin' after he were gone, and he went twice to free school. It kep' in three months, and Timothy allowed as that were schoolin' enough for anybody. Sammy were the smartest of all the children to work, and Timothy took to leavin' him a sight to do; but when he were fifteen he done told his Pa he wanted to buy his time off him, and go to the mission school at Hinkson's.

Say you ain't never heard tell of buyin' a boy's time off his Pa? Why, children *owes* their Pa their time 'til they're eighteen, for their board and clothes.

Sammy'd been such a peart one to work that he allowed he'd done a sight more'n his share; and so he had. He reckoned he could get work enough out of school time at Hinkson's to pay his Pa for the rest of his time. I done told Timothy he might as well let him go, for it weren't never no kind of use tryin' to cross Sammy when his mind were made up. He were always a right resolute child.

Timothy grumbled a sight when the boy were gone, 'count of there being; so much more work to do. Onct he borrowed a mule to go hisself and fetch him back. As luck would have it, a letter come from Sammy that very day. He'd sent his Pa some money in it, and writ that he'd send some more right soon. He said he done liked the school splendid, and were learnin' right smart. Timothy allowed he wouldn't go for him yet. Then the teacher's written as Sammy were such a good scollard, and hopin' we-uns meant to let him stay and get a eddication; so he kep' on. He done helped us a sight sendin' money he earned, but when he were eighteen he told his Pa he allowed he were free now, and he were goin' to do as his grandpop said.

Timothy hadn't nothin' to say agin' his goin' to Pennsylvany. He allowed as the boy'd maybe find some of Pa's folks up there right well-to-do, and they'd send us money, and we-uns wouldn't be down on our luck no more.

Chapter 2: Stepping Backwards

Sammy were growed such a peart young man, and he'd learned such pretty manners at school, and he wore such big red neckties, it done me good to look at him. I hated it bad to see him goin' way off, and like as not never come back.

He says to me: 'Don't you fret, Ma; you'll see me comin' back a rich man yet, and then you won't have to work so hard no more.' Sammy were a right good boy," said Mrs Simmons, wiping her eyes on her apron.

"And did he never come back?" I asked, sympathetically.

"No; I never sot eyes on him agin. He done found Pa's folks, real well-to-do farmers they was, and they set a sight of store by him. He done married one of their gals. Here's her picture," added Mrs. Simmons, blowing the dust from an old photograph which she took down from a shelf. "Here's their baby, too; ain't it a peart one? This here's Sammy," said she, taking an ambrotype from a box under the table. "This were took at Hinkson's, and he never got nary another one took."

He certainly did wear an immense red necktie, which the artist had touched up in color. An honest, boyish face looked out from the queer old picture, and I didn't wonder at his mother's emotion, if, as I supposed, he was dead.

"He died up there of pneumony fever," Mrs. Simmons presently resumed, in a broken voice. "His wife done wrote us how it were. About a year afterwards a letter came sayin' she were comin' to see us, but we ain't heard nary a word from her since. Do you allow as she's done married again?"

"Perhaps so," I replied, absently. I was wondering what the bright, well-dressed girl in the photograph would think of Sammy's home and people if she ever came to visit them.

"There ain't no one to send us no money since Sammy died. The rest on 'em ain't had no better luck nor their Pa. There's four of 'em; I buried two of the least ones. Sammy were a heap different from t'others. His dyin' were all of a piece with the rest of the bad luck we-uns has had. Never see nothin' like it. Nobody can't blame Timothy for gettin' so downhearted."

"Must you be goin'? I'm powerful glad you come by. You done me a sight o' good, bein so sorry about Sammy."

Chapter 3
A Foggy Day

Foggy Day

I

Toward the close of a showery spring day, I heard, through the fog which the mists rising from the valleys had heaped upon us, a high-pitched voice singing "My Way's Cloudy." The minor time accorded well with the steady drip, drip from the trees, the dismal croaking of the frogs in the meadow, and the weird color effects produced by the mist.

Presently the song ceased, the gate clanged, I heard steps on the path, and a dun-colored figure walked out of the fog. In bedraggled skirts and shoes heavy with mud, she looked of the earth earthy. A pleasant face topped the figure, however, and by way of greeting she said, cheerfully, "I brung you something." Depositing upon the grass as she spoke a bundle tied up in an old apron, she began at once to open it.

"I knowed how fond you be of wild flowers, so I dug you some roots. Me and Dan's been down to the river plantation workin' all day."

"Not in the rain!" I exclaimed.

"Yes; we've got to get our craps in, and it didn't rain so hard down there as they say it has up here. This here's *sang*. You-uns said you wanted to see what it were like. It's kind of hard to find now, for its nigh about dug out round here since the stores took to trading it to send to Chiny. Folks says them heathen Chinee *chaws* it! They must be mighty queer folks," continued Mrs. Ames, laughing, as she turned the quid of tobacco in her mouth.

"It's a sight how these here yaller lilies and this red horsemint grows if they get a chance. It's just beautiful to see 'em down to the

Chapter 3: Foggy Day

plantation when it comes blossoming time; you can't make no headway through 'em sometimes, they're so thick.

There ain't nothing I'm so fond of as flowers. I keep er bringing roots from the plantation, and plantin' 'em nigh the house, but, Lor'! there ain't no show for 'em, what with hogs and chickens and the men folks not keeping up the fences. There's a sight of pretties here. Get me a shovel, and I'll plant 'em for you."

Instead of accepting the kind offer, I took her into the house and made her a cup of coffee, for she still had a long walk before her.

Dropping into a chair, she pulled off her old sunbonnet, exclaiming: "I'm plum tired; I didn't know I were so wore out. The heart's kind of out of me, anyway; things has got all mixed up, and I can't see my way, nohow," she added, wearily.

"It's mighty peaceful and pretty down to the plantation," she said, after a pause. " 'Pears like my troubles ain't too heavy to tote down there. The river runs round the meadow-lots so pretty and free; you can hear it singin' over the stones and gurglin' like a baby some places. It's a heap of company when you're workin'. Sometimes, when I see the sticks and dead leaves a-swirlin' round on the water and bein' carried downstream, whether or no, I think they ain't much different from folks. Folks can't help theirselves any more than the leaves; they're just driftin' along, and 'tain't much use ketchin' on to things to hold back agin' the stream. I see some poor little fishes, as got left in pools by the last fresh. They 'minded me so of folks workin' round and round in places they can't never get out of, and ain't certain how they got into, neither, that I just *had to* put 'em back into the water," said Mrs Ames, with an apologetic laugh.

"I'm right queer that way, mixin' up things and folks in my head. I reckon some would allow I weren't all there, if I let on how I see things. It don't do to tell all a body thinks," she added, smiling brightly.

"The birds are plum lively down in the valley. I love to watch 'em building their nests; makes me think of young folks courtin'. I see a cute thing as I come along by the mill. There weren't nobody about, and there sot two ground squirrels on the hopper, jabbering away like they was folks. The sieve were atop of the hopper, so's they couldn't get nary a grain of corn, and they was that mad I had to laugh. But comin' along to the top of the mounting the fog got powerful thick, and it seemed like all my worriments come back on me."

"Was it you I heard singing?" I inquired.

"Yes; I learned that song when the niggers had camp meetin', and it helps me a sight when I'm down; I'm that way now. Did you say why? Oh! because everything's goin' wrong, and I can't see my way clear. Now, there's my Annie, her as I sent to Hinkson's to school, hopin' to make a teacher of her. I allowed she had a heap of sense, and I'd had such a sight of trouble with the rest that I were plum glad I didn't have to study about her. But, Lor'! young folks is all alike, I do believe. Gals is like birds a-settin on a bush waitin' for the fust boy that comes along to knock 'em off with a stone.

Nobody'd er thought my Annie would have looked at Tom Grogan. She always let on like she hated a feller what drinks and carries on like he does, and now she's plum crazy after him. Nary one of us daresn't say a word agin' him when she's about. She allows if she can't have him, she won't marry nobody; so we-uns give in to his coming to the house courtin' her. I'm nigh sick about it. My! but that's a pretty pink cup you're pourin' the coffee into," she exclaimed, brightening. "Annie's powerful fond of pretty things, and I've laid awake nights studyin' how to git 'em for her. I reckon she'll have to whistle for pretty things if she marries Tom Grogan. She's a right good scollard, but Tom can't even read. Gals is curious, and no mistake! Now, there's my Sarah Jane; I'm all beat out about her. She were bound to marry old Crosby, and him havin' four children, and she nothin' but a slip of a gal! He's cross-eyed, and that ugly to

Chapter 3: Foggy Day

look at 'peared like Dan and me just couldn't give in for her to have him, but she up and says, 'Why Ma, *you* ain't got to love him,' and no more we ain't. They've been married nigh on five year, and I ain't see nothin' to love about him yet; but they're having a hard time just now. He's one them unlucky kind as everything goes agin'. Sarah Jane ain't never been stout since her first baby came; she's got two, and is like for another. Poor folks has a sight of children. Old Crosby's by his first wife was all puny. They had six. If the Lord wanted 'em, I were glad they'd buried two of 'em before Sarah Jane got married. Them two gals of his is always ketchin' somethin'. Now it's the measles, and the whole tribe'll have 'em before they get through. As if that wasn't enough, what does old Crosby hisself go and do last week but let a log roll atop of him. He's been in bed ever since, groanin' and hollerin', but he won't have no doctor. I wanted Annie to go and stay with 'em while things was so bad, but she allows it makes her sick the nasty way they live. Besides, she says Sarah Jane's served just right for marrying a no-'count man! I wish she'd take warnin', but 'tain't no use wishin'. She's on the edge of the nest, and she allows she knows how to fly; so she's bound to go over," Mrs. Ames added, in a voice robbed of its usual cheerfulness.

"Bill's wife's puny this spring, too. I can't help studyin' about 'em all. If I could be in two or three places at once, I shouldn't feel so bad. Agin I do my own work and the milkin', and work in the craps, I'm plum wore out, and a body's got to get *some* sleep. Dan, he's sort of puny, too, and a heap of times he can't even chop wood, so I have it to do."

I asked what part of the work Annie did.

"Oh, she hates to work; that's why I 'lowed to make a scollard of her, so she wouldn't have nothin' to do. She gets peaked the least bit of hard work she does. She can't even carry water for me when I'm doin' boarders' wash without it givin' her a hurtin' in her breast. Yes, she sews some. She likes her things fixy, but she ain't got no time for mending," added Mrs. Ames, glancing at her own shabby attire. "If she marries Tom Grogan, she'll be lucky if she even has things to mend. It's all mighty bad, but the Lord made me so's I always see the funny side of things. It's been a heap of help to me sometimes. It is funny to see gals as can't do no work at home marrying no-'count men that they have to pick right up and carry. I wish it was some other gal besides my Annie as were sot on doing it, though.

There's other things pestering me, too. We-uns owes fifty dollars on our house, and Mr. Screw holds the papers. They're run out, and he allows he can't wait no longer for his money, so he's fixin' to sell us out. I had thirty dollars saved up towards it, but I couldn't see Sara Jane and the rest so down on their luck, and not give 'em a lift. It's been a right hard winter for us, anyway. Our other gal Jessie's been at home with her baby and her old man since the first of the year. He's a right well-meanin' man, but he don't have no luck. 'Peared like things was goin' agin' him right along; so the man he rented his place from allowed he'd take if off his hands, and he give up and brung his family to our house. We-uns is pinched for room, and Annie don't like it. She says mean things to Brad; that's Jessie's man. I feel plum sorry for him sometimes. Things seem all in a muddle, somehow; leastways, that's how I feel now. I don't see no light nowheres."

Rising stiffly to her feet, she put on her old sunbonnet, saying: "I must go 'long home and milk. Here I been settin' enjoying myself, and forgettin' that them poor things won't git a bite of supper ready 'til I'm there to help. It'll be plum dark agin I get the milkin' done.

I'm obleeged to you for the coffee and snack. They've heartened me up a sight. I reckon it's goin' to clear; it don't seem nigh so thick at it did when I come in," said Mrs. Ames, as she disappeared in the enveloping cloud.

At sunset the fog, suddenly lifting, floated away in vapor. A dripping world tossed back his own radiance into the face of the sun when he burst forth, while the mountains glowed like burnished copper 'til twilight drew it's purple veil.

Chapter 3: Foggy Day

II

At Evening Time It Shall Be Light

The plants brought to me by Mrs. Ames that foggy day were growing thriftily, some of them were already in bloom; for the spring was behind us, and we were in the heart of an unusually warm and dry summer. In consequence of the water-courses getting low, there was much sickness, and I heard one day that Mrs. Ames, among others, was "down with the fever." The next afternoon I was shocked to receive a message that she was "about to die," and wanted to see me.

I found her looking terribly ill, but the old cheerful smile illumined her face as she recognized me and feebly put out her hand to take mine. When I told her the bunch of red mint I had just laid on her pillow came from the roots she had brought me, she said, softly: "Ain't it queer how *things* outlasts folks? Them flowers will go on bloomin' when I'm plum forgot."

"Did you see the doctor as you come in?" she asked; and then continued, slowly: "He set quiet holding my wrist, and after a bit I see him wipin' his eyes, and he says, smoothin' my hair like I were a little gal, 'I'm plum sorry I can't do no more for you, Mrs. Ames; it makes me feel bad.'

'You ain't no call to blame yourself, Doctor,' I says. 'There's been a heap o' times you done helped me when you didn't even know it. Many's the time it done me good just to meet up with you, 'count of your kind ways. Sick and well, we-uns has had a sight of help from you; so you must just set this off agin' that.' "

"I laughed," said she, "but I see tears in his eyes. 'We'll miss your pleasant ways, Mrs. Ames,' he says, and that brung the tears into my eyes, too."

Waiting a few moments to recover breath, she went on more slowly: "He'd er helped me if anybody could, but I reckon I'm like that old clock up there," she added, with a pathetic little laugh. "'Machinery's wore out,' the tinker said. Just before it quit goin' for good it took to buzzing so the baby were scared, and all the strikes went off at once, and it ain't budged since."

"Tell 'em not to cry," she whispered, pointing to a group of her family and friends, weeping audibly at the foot of the bed. "It frets me to hear 'em; I'm wore out, and I need quiet. There ain't nothin' to cry about. It's all clear as day before me. It's like I'd been workin' hard one the them long, foggy days, when everything were all mixed up and hard to understand, and there weren't no light nowheres." She paused a moment for breath. "Now it's evenin'; the fog's lifted and the sun's settin'; he's just *burstin' out*, and it's all light and bright. Everything's shining with glory!"

She closed her eyes, resting a few moments. Then the failing voice went on: "Do you remember how you read me about Christian dropping his pack at the cross, and how happy he were when he got shut of it? I'm like that now. I done toted all their loads," she whispered, glancing affectionately at her weeping family, "'til I were plum broke down. Long while back the doctor told me my lungs was weak, and when I took pneumony fever I knowed it weren't no more use, and I just let the whole pack roll off me, like Christian did. I'm so thankful to be layin' here restin', just waitin' on the Lord's will. It's hard on them, poor things," she murmured, her eyes filling with tears; "but I reckon the Lord knows what's best."

At this the weeping broke forth afresh, and she closed her eyes wearily. Dan, the picture of woe, stood at the head of the bed, keeping off the flies with a laurel branch. The tears rolled down his thin cheeks, nesting unheeded in his scraggy beard, but he uttered no sound to disturb his dying mate.

Presently she spoke again. "I ain't much account, nohow, but I done the best I could; and the Lord knows better than folks does how hard-pushed I've been most times. I've been like the sticks and leaves whirlin' and driftin' down the stream. I fought agin' it a sight, but 'long to the last I see it weren't no use; so I just give in to drift. They say the river's carryin' of 'em down to the sea.

I don't know nothing about the sea I'm driftin' to, but I'm in the still waters now, and I ain't afraid to trust the Lord. He's been mighty good to me, and give me a heap of blessings I weren't half thankful enough for. I see a sight er worriment all my life, but I weren't never one of them as looks long on the dark side, and that's been a heap of help to me and the rest. I 'lowed you'd read me agin that chapter in the Bible about peace," she said, faintly, after a long pause.

Annie got the Bible, and I read the fourteenth chapter of St. John, while the sick woman lay with closed eyes and folded hands, a look of great peace upon her shrunken face. As I closed the book, I could see through the open door the shadows grown long and the underside of the leaves of the great white rhododendron that grew by the little porch silvering in the rays of the setting sun.

"Now sing me them verses I liked so well of the hymn you played for me Sunday were two weeks," said the fast failing voice.

It had been hard for me to read calmly, and I waited for command of my voice to sing. Opening her eyes, the dying woman whispered feebly: "Don't feel bad; you wouldn't if you knowed how happy I be, and how bright and clear it all is."

So I swallowed hard, and began softly singing her favorite verses of "Sun of My Soul," watching her the while, as she lay on her miserable bed, the embodiment of peace. As I began the last verse, her eyes opened suddenly with a smile into mine. A swift change passed over her face, and ere I finished the last line I knew she was already afloat upon that sea towards which she had rejoiced to feel herself drifting.

Mr. Timmins

A search for health landed us among the North Carolina mountains. Spring was at hand, and nothing could exceed the beauty of the external world, to which the languorous sighing of the pines and the joyous notes of mating birds seemed to give voice. It was like watching from a distance the approach of a friend to see the tender green of the budding trees start in the coves and valleys, and climb slowly up the mountain sides, to burst at last into sudden glory of leaf and bloom at the top.

Our new neighbors and their primitive methods of life and work interested us greatly.

On one of the our long drives we came across an old man chopping wood near where we camped at noon, and we invited him to share our lunch. He proved a very entertaining guest. After showing us the old cabin where he and his wife lived alone, he gave us a sketch of his life, much of which, naively told, was very interesting.

"I reckon you-uns wasn't livin' round these parts war times," said he. "I were. We-uns seen a sight o' worriment them days. My people was all for the Union, so I slipped off and jined the Union army.

The war's over long ago, and them as fit in it ain't got nary a grudge agin' nobody. They likes to tell, when they git together, how they used to call one another Yanks and Rebs, and swap tobacco and hard-tack whenever there were a flag o' truce, and to brag how they fit and licked each other. Them kind don't stir up no contention. They done had enough of it war times. It's them as were all talk and bluster then as goes on the same way now. I weren't never one of them contentious sort. All I want is a chance to work and live peaceable. Life ain't long enough to be always pesterin' about what a body ain't no call to meddle with.

My brother Bill weren't so strong as me, and he staid to home to help Ma. The home guard, as they done called theirselves, shot him, 'cause they couldn't make him tell where I were at. He weren't never no 'count for work agin. They done served a sight that way.

My father died when I were little, and Ma seen hard times raisin' us young 'uns. Bill and me done a heap o' work to help her along, but when the war come on she allowed as one of us ought to fight for the country, so I went, being the strongest. I kept a-studyin' about t'others while I were away, though, and sure enough, when I come back, poor Ma were dead and gone, and Bill plum broke down. Ma weren't never to say strong, and she overdone herself after Bill were shot.

Them home guards run off folks' cattle, too. We'd kept our cow by hidin' of her down in a cove, but when she were a-calvin' she were like to die, and Ma allowed it weren't worth while to let her die now, after all the bother we'd had keepin' of her so long. Ma knowed a right smart about sick-nursin'. The neighbors used to send after her from all around for sickness. When night come on and Ma seen the cow weren't no better, she come back to the house and done told Bill and the gals she reckoned she'd set up with her.

They was plum set agin' her doin' it, and the gals allowed they'd set up and Ma go to bed. She wouldn't hear to it, though. She knowed how skeery they be, and she done told 'em to quit talkin', for she were bent on doin' her duty by that poor cow. It were a cold night, and she daresn't make no fire, 'count of somebody maybe seein' it, but she took along Pa's old lantern under her shawl. The gals allowed they hadn't never seen the stars so bright, but there weren't no moon.

Ma done saved the cow, but when she didn't come home in the mornin' the gals went to find her, and there she sot, plum dead."

"Not your poor mother?" I asked, hoping that Mr. Timmins had got things mixed and meant the cow.

"Yes, poor Ma," he replied. "The gals come on her settin' there that natural and pretty, with her sunbonnet on, they allowed she were asleep. Them were bad time for we-uns, and they lost the cow for all. Ma's dying in the cove put the home guards on the scent, and the next day the cow and calf was gone."

Playing With Fire

On one of my long walks in early spring I came upon a little cabin in the valley, and recognized an acquaintance standing in the doorway. It was Mrs. Rastus Barns. She urged my coming in to rest before climbing the hill again.

"You-uns ain't been used to the mountings, and you'll be plum broke down and wore out 'fore you get back," she said, "if you don't set awhile."

The bare trees and ever-green rhododendrons, standing up against the bluest of skies, made a lovely picture, as I glanced back over the way I had come, but the path seemed steep and long. As I hesitated, I realized that I was tired; so I went in with Mrs. Barns, and sat by the door on a straight-backed splint chair.

Presently I asked her if she and her neighbor did not find their one-roomed houses too small for comfort.

"We git used to 'em," she replied, smiling. "I reckon you-uns was raised different, so they look queer to you. I *were* awful pestered when Sal were a corpse though."

"Who was Sal?" I asked, startled by this sudden introduction of a cadaver.

"She were my youngest sister," answered Mrs. Barns. "Sal weren't rightly her name. Ma named her Meranthy Angeliny, outin' a book she heard read. Ma and Pa hadn't no chance to git a eddication, and they couldn't neither of 'em read.

When Sal got so's she could talk, t'others was plaguin' her one day about havin' sich a long name. She allowed as that weren't her name, nohow. She said her right name were Sal, and after that she wouldn't answer to none other. So we-uns give in to call her Sal. She were a mighty pesterin' young 'un. She weren't all there, and she nigh about wore Ma out. I took her to live along o' we-uns after

Ma died, but she were a sight o' worriment. I never see no one, from that to this, that could be in so many places at once as it 'peared like Sal could.

One day Pa and Rastus was burnin' down a tree that had fell over and got stuck in a big oak; so they done sot it afire to make it fall. They was goin' to the mill, so they come to the house for the corn Sal and me had shelled for 'em. Sal weren't no 'count for work, but she were right spry at shellin' corn. She'd carry some of it round with her, and have every hog and chicken on the place follerin' of her. Then she'd fire the cobs at 'em, and laugh fit to kill herself if she hit one.

When the men folks was goin' to the mill, Pa says to me, 'Sis, you keep a eye on Sal, so she don't go nigh the big tree.' Rastus says to her; 'Now, Honey, you stay right here 'long o'sis 'til I git back, and I'll fetch you some o' them molasses." She said she would, and they done went along.

I were powerful busy washin' and bilin' soap that mornin'. 'Pears like men folks always had to go to the mill or somewhere just when they might be some help at home. The baby were that cross cuttin' teeth you 'a' heard him holler clean to the settlemint. I had him layin' on a pallet under a tree. I kept runnin' 'twixt him and the wash and the soap, but I hadn't no call to go to the house. The last time I were in, I see Sal were all right, with her chew-stick and snuff, and playin' with the cat. Then I plum forgot her.

The baby went off to sleep, and I settled down peaceable to my work, and never give a thought to Sal and the old tree. The birds was a-singin', and I heard the young lambs a-bleatin', and the wind stirrin' in the trees, and the sky were so blue, and the clouds so white and woolly, that it rested me just to be out of doors.

Washin' and soap-bilin' is powerful hard work when you have to carry all the wood for the fires, and like as not chop it, too. Women folks sees hard times in the mountings.

Chapter 5: Playing With Fire

Well, Pa and Rastus come 'long home jest as I were puttin' away the tubs, and feelin' good 'count o' bein' so nigh through. 'Where's Sal?' Pa says first thing. 'In the house,' says I; 'but mind you don't wake the baby; he's done hollered and cried most ever since you-uns went to the mill. Looks cute layin' there asleep, don't he?' I says. Pa were a-standin' right 'long side o' the pallet, and it made me laugh to see how the baby favored his grandpop.

Pa and Rastus done carried in the meal, and then they come runnin' out o' the door, like they was scared, and cut for the old tree. I run to the house, and I see Sal were gone, and before I got to the door agin I heard sich a shout! I can't never forget it.

I ain't one of them fainty kind, but I had to lean hard agin' the doorpost, and when I got so's I could see, there were Pa and Rastus bringin' somethin' heavy to the house. I knowed right away what it were, and I had to set down on the floor just where I were at.

Sal, not havin' right sense, must a' stood lookin' up into the tree 'til it fell atop her, an' she never drawed another breath. I were glad to think she couldn't a' suffered, for I blamed myself a sight for not keepin' a watch on her. You see, I'd put out the fire in the stove before I come out, so I knowed there weren't no fire for her to fool with. We always had to keep the matches hid from her too.

Did you say were she fond of playing with fire? She were that. Onct before she come nigh burnin' up. Pa and Ma were out in the field hoein' corn, and they'd left Sal asleep in the house, and they thought the the fire were out. Pa reckoned he'd go to the spring for a drink. It's plum curious how thirsty some men is they get a job of work to do. It beats all to see how many times they have to go to the spring. It would wear 'em all out to go that often for water to cook with.

Well, Pa allowed he'd better look into the house and see if Sal were all right. There she were, a'sweepin' the floor with one o' them brush brooms, and it, and her, too was all afire. Pa had brung a bucket o' water from the spring that trip, and he quick throwed it over her and put out the fire, and scared poor Sal nigh to death. She were plum afraid o' water, and wouldn't go nigh it if she could help herself. She wouldn't even wash her own face and hands, and she hollered when you done it for her.

We-uns always had to watch out for her about fire, though, so it ain't no wonder she come to a fiery end, is it?"

"No," I replied; "but you haven't told me yet why your one-roomed house was so uncomfortable when your sister died."

"Well, it were along o' the way the neighbors come and come and come when they heard about Sal, 'til I were nigh about crazy, the house were so full," Mrs. Barns replied. "Some on 'em brung their young 'uns to larn 'em a lesson, they said, seein' as most was heady like Sal about gettin' their own way. Them children cried and went on fit to waken the corpse, and my baby were scared of 'em all. He were that cross I couldn't set him down a minute. It come on to rain, too, and that made it worse.

'Peared like Sal were the only one had any room. They all fit shy o' her, layin' there under a sheet on the bed in the corner. The men folks allowed as there weren't nothin' for it but to git the funeral over with; so they sot up all night makin' Sal's coffin. It sounded mighty lonesome to hear 'em hammerin' and sawin' on sich work after it got dark, and I were right glad Mr. and Mis' Jones brung their pallet and slept on the floor.

There were a owl hootin' in the woods, and a dog howlin', and Mis' Jones 'lowed as that meant another death. Pa Jones says to her, 'Ma, them critters is right over nigh our house,' and she done shut up.

Preacher Smith were holdin' a 'tracted meetin' at the Baptist Church. He come over next mornin' and said a prayer, and we buried Sal nigh Ma's grave in the old field. We was that wore out when it were all over I reckon we'd a' slept a week if it weren't for the baby hollerin' for his breakfast.

Chapter 5: Playing With Fire

Them mayflowers you got in your hand puts me in mind o' that time," said Mrs. Barns. "'Peared like Sal done picked a sight of 'em before she set nigh the old tree. They was all strowed round where she were layin'. The neighbors gathered 'em up, and we put 'em on the coffin along o' Sal. She were right fond o' flowers. She looked more peacefuller layin' in her coffin than I'd ever see her. Even when she were asleep, she were like to holler out or jump up. You had to sleep with one eye open to watch her. You couldn't never tell what she'd do.

I were thinkin' o' her when I see you comin'. I were lookin' at them there trees way down in the holler. I disremember their names, but I ain't never see 'em white like that since the year Sal died."

I looked where she pointed. In the depths of the valley, where the stream had, as she expressed it, "quit its hurry," a group of moulted sycamores stood forth ivory-white in the sunshine.

"Look sort o' like ghosts, don't they?" Mrs. Barns said, smiling. Then, she added, "I think them beeches up above 'em's a sight prettier."

The hillside showed the gray of bare beeches, some drooping long arms and dipping slender branches almost to earth.

"'Pears like some trees is a heap nicer than others to look at in winter," she said. "Beeches is that way. A sight o' leaves hangs on 'em nigh all winter, and them that draps is right yaller. Cloudy days it looks like the sun were shinin' round 'em. Oaks is nice to look at in winter, too, but they's more browner."

"What a beautiful tree!" I exclaimed, calling her attention to a noble white pine on the hillside.

"Know the reason, don't ye?" she responded, quickly. "That's 'count of it's growin' in the clearin'. Look at them trees in that piece o' wood yonder. Ain't nary one of 'em but what's growed crooked or queer someways. Some on 'em's scarce grow'd at all, 'count o'bein so crowded up together. It's that way with folks. A sight of 'em ain't never had no room to stretch in. That kind's mighty apt to get crabbed when they's old. That's what's the matter with a heap o' children; their folks don't never let 'em alone a minute. I stepped into Mis' Travers' yesterday, and the way she kept after them young 'uns o' hers was a sight. She were a-flyin' out at 'em every minute. Even Saludy, the biggest gal, come in for a slap before I come away, and she's goin' on seventeen. Ain't one o' them young 'uns but holds it's head kind o' queer, like it were dodgin' a blow. I declare I were afraid I'd catch the same trick if I staid there long. Mis' Travers hadn't let them young 'uns alone a single minute whilst I were there, and when I see her goin' for Saludy I reckoned I'd staid long enough. I weren't sure she wouldn't git round to me next," Mrs. Barns said, laughing. "We-uns wasn't raised that way. My people was poor, but they was right peaceable."

When I was leaving, I gave her part of my bunch of trailing arbutus. "'Bleeged to you for these," said she; "I'll put 'em on Sal's grave. I ain't got time to go huntin' 'em myself."

Chapter 6
Neighborly Gossip

Neighborly Gossip

One day when I called at Mrs. Lank's, I found her at her loom, which darkened the only window the house could boast of.

After showing me the blue-and-white spread she was weaving, she seemed glad to leave her work for a friendly chat.

"Weavin's tiresomer work than you'd think," said she, seating herself near the fire, and taking down her hair as she talked. This was a pet habit of hers, but it always came upon me as a diverting surprise. Such a head of hair as she had! It was long, light, and so slippery – slick, she called it – that no hairpins that were ever invented could keep it in order long.

"A body's got to look mighty sharp to keep track o' the pattern in one o' them spreads," she resumed, thickly, with her mouth full of hairpins. "And you git tired all over settin' workin' the loom. I'm right glad you come by, so's I can rest a bit. My! but you-uns set's a heap o' store by them ivy blossoms," said Mrs. Lank, referring to the bunch of mountain laurel in my hand. "Why, they're plenty as dirt."

"Yes, but they're so beautiful," I protested. "They'd brighten your room wonderfully if you'd fill that old crock in the corner with them."

"'Lor me! I ain't got no time for no sich foolishness," she replied, taking the hairpins out of her mouth and putting them into her hair.

Then she asked: "Did you hear about the row Mr. and Mis' Patty's been havin'? Say you ain't? Well, it's just a sight the way them two goes on. Last I heard he done beat her. I wouldn't stand a beatin' from no man – no, not if he was a gold man!" said Mrs. Lank, giving her head a toss that sent the hairpins flying. "He drinks, but some allows as he's drove to it by the way she behaves. The church members has been wantin' to have her up before the church, and now they're all argufying about it. Some on 'em allows if she's

Chapter 6: Neighborly Gossip

let off they'll take their letters and go over to the Baptists. There's a heap o' them Methodys, anyway, that ain't plum sure in their minds as sprinklin's safe. Some on 'em done told me they git right low in their minds about it sometimes. They reckon they'd feel a heap safer if they'd been soused, but they jined at the big 'tracted meetin'. There was more'n forty a-mournin at onct, and thirty jiners. I never see sich a sight. Folks got all worked up, cryin' and goin' on. Miss Brand went up and down, cryin' and wringin' her hands. 'Peared like she allowed as everybody but her were goin' straight to the bad place. She kept a hollerin' for the Lord to save her nevvy, Aleck Burr. She went and grabbed holt of him, and tried to drag him to the mourner's bench, but he dodged, and him and t'other boys he were with run out," Mrs. Lanks said, laughing.

"Preacher Crosby got mighty worked up, too, shoutin' louder and louder, 'til he were frothin' at the mouth like a dumb critter. He's a right good man, but some on 'em ain't got no use fore him 'count o' his bein' so down on liquor and 'stillin'.

They ain't never had another o' them big 'tracted meetin's, and Preacher Crosby allows as a sight of 'em's fell away from grace since. Fact is," said she, lowering her voice confidentially, "folks gits tired o' one preacher, and havin' him jaw at 'em about their sins. Besides, they grudge payin' Mr. Crosby seventy-five dollars a year, when they might get another man for fifty. They reckon he's too much after the make. That's 'count of his sayin' no man couldn't right'y study Scriptur' and preach acceptable unto the Lord when he had to work so hard as he done on the farm to support his family. His wife's weakly most times, and two o' their young'uns is puny.

Did you say couldn't we give him more salary? Well, some o' the church members is right well-to-do, but they'se mighty nigh when it comes to money."

Just then a man with lantern jaws appeared in the doorway. He stood with gaping mouth, waiting for Mrs. Lank to ask his errand.

He wanted her husband. She said he was at the mill, and the man went away.

Mrs. Lank laughed. "I can't never see Tom Booth," she said, "without thinkin' of the time t'other fellers put him up to keepin' company with me. I couldn't abide him, and they knowed it; but they let on to him like I were sweet on him. He came up with me, bold as brass, goin' home from preachin' one night."

Here Mrs. Lank threw back her head and laughed so heartily that away flew her hairpins, and the second arrangement of her hair went for naught.

"When I see it were him, I *were* mad!" she resumed. "I says to him: 'If you're bound to go 'long home with me, Tom Booth, I'll get Pop to make you a clamp to keep your mouth shut,' I says. Pop were a blacksmith.

Tom looked like I'd struck him. He never said a word, but he turned short round and went after the Dent gals. He done married one of 'em. Him and me was bad friends and never spoke for a long time after that. Afterwards he allowed I'd spoke unthoughted, and he said he hadn't no grudge agin' me. Nobody ever see him with his mouth shut, and he snores terrible," said she, smiling. "Time his sister that lived with him died, him and Katy was plum wore out takin' care of her. Me and two other gals offered to set up all night with the corpse and let them folks sleep. And you'd oughter heard 'em sleep. One played bass and the t'other trible. They kept us laughin' so we hadn't no trouble keepin' awake, nor no chance to get skeery. Lor' me!" said Mrs Lank, lapsing into a vein of reminiscence, "that set me back to when I were young. Gals is queer. I reckon I weren't no different from t'others. 'Pears like I were always laughing at somethin' or other them days. A body ain't no call to laugh so much when they get older.

Maybe you wouldn't believe it, but I were a right good-lookin' gal. I had a sight o' sweethearts. The feller's all wanted me for partner at corn-shuckin's. Me and Mr. Hawley was keepin' company when I were seventeen," Mrs. Lank added, in a tone which showed that she expected me to be much impressed by this bit of information. Mr. Hawley stood high in the community because of his worldly success. Morally he was a miserable failure, however.

Mrs. Lank continued: "My folks wouldn't give in to our marryin' though. He were a poor boy then. He got mad and went away to Georgy. He were the only man I were ever really in love with. I never see him agin 'til he come back here after his second wife died. I were married myself then, and anyways, he'd got too biggotty for sich as me.

Did you say weren't I in love with my man when I married him? 'Bout like common. We got along all right. He were in love with another gal, too. Her folks wouldn't hear to their marryin'; so him an' me got married to spite our folks," she said, with a short laugh.

"Yes, there were a chance that we might a spited ourselves worser, but we're both mighty easy goin', so we get on together well as most folks. Land! where's my hairpins gone to?" Mrs. Lank exclaimed, abruptly, as she began groping about the dim room in search of them.

When she had recovered the strays, she sat down and began upon her hair again.

Presently she said: "I don't guess you stopped to see old Mr. Mason as you come along? He's right bad off."

"No; I didn't know he was ill," I replied.

"Oh, he ain't ill," she returned, hastily.

"He's always been right good to his folks, and a lamb couldn't be patienter nor him now he's sick. No, he weren't never ill. He's sufferin' a sight, a kind o' suffocatin'; can't get his breath. The room's plum full o' the neighbors settin' round. The doctor allowed as them that wasn't no help to the family had oughter go away, so I come home. He done told 'em they was spoilin' what air there were to breathe, and the poor old man couldn't get enough, nohow. Some on 'em got mad, and for spite they done told Mis' Mason the doctor said her man was dyin' right then. The poor thing come outside, where Mr. Mason couldn't hear her, and she took on powerful. But I heard what the doctor said, and it weren't no sich as that. I done told her so. He said you might as well give a sick body pisen to drink as to pisen the only air he's got to breathe. I ain't smart enough to understand no sich, but I know he's a right good doctor. Since he's come here folks don't die with the fever like they done before."

"Well, did the neighbors go home!" I asked.

"Me and some others come away, but a sight of 'em staid, and I reckon Mis' Mason and the gals had to cook dinner for 'em," Mrs. Lank replied.

"Poor old Mr. Mason has seen a sight o' worriment, 'long o'bad children and bad health. Him and her's always been right steady-goin' and peaceable, but it 'pears like their boys and gals is always up to some devilment. There's bad stock on the mother's side. She were one o'them Cole bastards, and it's comin' out the children. It's apt to. Some folks seen a heap o' worriment, don't they?" said she, putting finishing touches to her hair as she sat by the dingy hearth, which looked as if it had never scraped acquaintance with a broom. The very fire seemed to burn dimly in this unkempt room. Good housekeeping was not one of Mrs. Lank's virtues, evidently.

"Preacher reckons as them that has it hard here'll git it made up to 'em in heaven. I don't know how 'tis," she added, thoughtfully. "I've studied a heap about it. Now, there's old Mr. Mason; his two oldest boys went straight to bad. They was both killed in a drunken fight. Many's the time I see him just a-humpin to work, and them boys off on some devilment or other.

They done spoiled 'em when they's little, for one thing. Preacher Crosby allows as a little birch-tea's a heap better'n pettin' sometimes. I don't guess he's fur wrong, neither," she added, readjusting her hairpins. Mr. Mason set a heap o' store by them boys, and he ain't never quit grievin' about their dyin' in their sins. Mis' Mason says he even talks about it in his sleep. Many's the time I've heard him say there couldn't be no heaven for him without them two boys, and if the Lord'd let him, he'd go to the bad place right cheerful, and serve out their time for 'em, so's they'd be sot free. Them's the things I just can't see can be made up. Can you?" she asked, wistfully.

I knew she had similar troubles of her own, although she had never spoken of them to me.

"I don't think they can," I replied. "But why should we believe of our Heavenly Father what we would not for a moment believe of our earthly parents? Do you think God could be less loving and forgiving toward those two boys than their own father is?"

"I ain't heard tell o' no sich pint o' view," said Mrs. Lank, suspiciously, putting up her hand absently to feel if it was the slipping of her troublesome back hair that had given her an unsettled feeling.

At that moment a neighbor hurried in to says that Mr. Mason was dead, and Mrs Mason wanted Mrs. Lank to help to lay him out.

I gave her my bunch of laurel for the house of mourning.

As I passed out of that cheerless room into the sunshine, I could almost imagine the joy of release to the soul whose troubles we had just been discussing.

Chapter 7: Barter

Barter

I

When I gave Mrs. Hapgood a lift in the buggy because she was carrying a heavy load, she began at once to tell me her "business to the settlemint."

"I toted a big load to the store this mornin'," she said. "We-uns gathers a sight o' roots and yarbs and other things for barter. Miss Blane done carried my big sack part way on her mule, or I wouldn't be gittin' back so soon."

It was now four o'clock. She had given up the better part of a day to her business transactions in the way of barter. The subject of barter interested me greatly. Hearsay had it that the shopkeepers always came out ahead, so I liked to hear the other side state the case. Mrs. Hapgood was garrulous, and I encouraged her to run on.

"I had other things besides roots and yarbs," she said; "I had a sight of beeswax, and they pay right smart for that. We-uns keeps bees. We smoke 'em with sulphur and kill 'em when we want to take the honey. We get a heap of wax that way. Yes, I reckon it's bad kill'n of 'em off so; we done had six stands, and now we ain't got but two left. Folks' bees always swarm in the spring, though, and if you watch out sharp you kin often catch a stray swarm. I worked a whole day last spring ringin' bells and things to catch one, and didn't get it after all. Peter even clomb the tree they was on, but they up and flew away. We'd have had a sight of bees by this time if ours hadn't got burned up when our house were burned. Peter's father give us two nice stand of bees in new bee-gums when we was married, and we had six setting close to the house that day.

Him and me had been over to his Pa's spending the day. Before we went we watered out the fire in the fireplace and covered it up, and we found it just like we left it; so it weren't that as sot the fire. We reckoned it were along of our having bees so close. There were a simple feller going about then as had a powerful big sweet tooth, and folks allowed as he knowed we was gone, and come pesterin' the bees to get some honey. 'Tain't likely he had any sulphur, and maybe he tried smokin' 'em with tobacco. That maken 'em plum wild. If they stung him, he'd drop the fire and run. Like as not that's what he done, and it ketch'd in the dry leaves laying about. It were a dry time. Fire's easy sot, but it's plum hard to ketch up with when it gets goin'. Me and Peter see the smoke when we was comin' home. We allowed it were some on 'em burnin' brush, and we wished folks weren't so free to set out fires such dry times. When we come out into the clearing and see it were our own house, we both hollered and took to runnin'. He were carrying a basket of good things – sassages, pies, and sich – his Ma done gave him. We never know'd what become of 'em, but we reckoned the hogs did," she said, laughing, "I were totin' the baby. I were always right careful of her. I have to laugh, though, when I think how I done served her that time. I see Peter's wagon standin' there, and as luck would have it, there were straw in the bottom of it, but it would have been all the same if it were bare. I up and give the baby a toss into the wagon as I run by, and never looked to see what she lit on. All I knowed was that she couldn't get out. The way she hollered were a caution, though we didn't take notice to it 'til afterwards. All him and me was thinkin' was could we save our things; but it were too late to get out much. It were a big loss to young married folks and mighty disheartenin'.

But we couldn't keep from laughin', after it were all over, to see that young 'un. She were kickin' and squallin', with her fists full of straw. She kept pokin' it into her eyes and mouth, and that made her madder than ever," added Mrs. Hapgood, laughing heartily at the recollection.

"There's a sight of fires among the mountings. Folks allows as most of 'em's set for spite by your enemies. What with religion and

Chapter 7: Barter

politics, a body's like to have a lot of enemies. If a man's a Dimocrat, and his house burns down, he allows as the 'Publicans done it. Same way, if he's a 'Publican, he allows as the Dimocrats done it. It's just so about religion, too. If he's a Methody, he reckons that Baptists done it; if he's a Baptist, he's plum sure it were the Methodys, or like as not the Presbyterians, and he won't hear to nothin' else. Folks is always argufyin' and quarrelin' about such as that. Sometimes it comes to out-and-out fightin', but most times it's just meanness. There's seven kind of Baptists in the mountings, and some on 'em's nigh to a fight every time they come together.

But when there's a fire, the neighbors all turn out, enemies or no enemies, and save all they can. When Mr. Blank's house were burned, they sot the things out and kept goin' in for more 'til he just begged 'em to quit, fear of the roof fallin' on 'em. A sight of 'em was down on him, too, 'count of his being a 'Publican. Folks likes to talk, though; 'pears like a heap of 'em would bust if they couldn't take the lid off that way sometimes."

I reminded Mrs. Hapgood that she had not finished telling me about her trade at the store.

"Sure enough," she exclaimed, with one of her ready laughs. "I reckon you think I'm one of them that don't know enough to put the lid on when it's off. Peter says my tongue's a sight when it's waggin'. What was it you asked me? Oh yes; about my trade at the store. I had a heap of things. I only got five cents a dozen for my eggs, and six cent's a pound for my butter. It were right good too, But Mr. Sill said it were too white lookin'. I done sot the cream too nigh the fire, and that hurt it. Mr. Sill writ down on a paper all the things I brung. I ain't no scollard myself. He done counted 'em all up to make sure it were all right, and told me what they come to. He asked were I satisfied, and I allowed I were bound to be. It did seem mighty little, though, after the way I'd worked to get 'em together and the long ways I'd toted 'em. The fact is, poor folks ain't got much chance. A

63

body's plum tired after totin' a load to the store, and they're willin' to strike most any kind of a bargain to get shut of it.

Some of 'em takes their children along, too. It's a sight of worriment; they come along so slow and pesterin'. The least ones gets so tired you're bound to have to tote 'em, atop of everything else. I make mine stay at home. I've brung 'em some candy. They knowed I would. Here it is; take some," said Mrs. Hapgood, producing a newspaper parcel and offering me some of the most villainously colored cheap candy I had ever beheld. I declined with thanks, suggesting at the same time that it should be given to the children homeopathically.

"Don't nothing hurt my children," Mrs. Hapgood replied, with a laugh. "They do have colic a sight though. What do I give' em for the colic, did you say? I give 'em catnip tea, with a heap of honey, or tree sugar, one, in it; that's the only way I can git 'em to touch it. It mostly always cures 'em.

Yes, I took in a sight of yarbs to the store. I disremember 'em all now. We-uns gathers a heap of 'em on the full of the moon. Folks allows as that makes 'em better. There was all kinds of roots, too, the kinds the doctors use for medicine. There must be a sight of sickness up North. That's where Mr. Sill says he sends 'em all. He says the freight costs a heap, and they's why he don't give no more for 'em. We-uns used to dig sang, and get big money for it, but it's nigh about all dug up round here now.

I were plum loaded down goin' in, but all I brung back were this bag of flour and what's in this basket. First-off, there was shoes to get for me and Janey. She's my biggest one. I been tellin' her I allowed she'd get a new dress for sure this lick. But I couldn't make it out. We-uns has to have coffee and tobacco. My old man uses a sight o' chewin' tobacco."

"But surely you don't use tobacco?" I ventured to remark.

Chapter 7: Barter

"I dip snuff," said she, producing her snuff-box. "Then there's bakin'-powder and sody," she continued, examining the contents of her basket. "Them's molasses in that there can. This her's a bag of white flour. That costs a sight, but Peter's a great hand for sody biscuits. He gets dreadful tired of cornmeal and buckwheat. I got this piece of fat meat for him, too, 'cause our hog meat's give out. That's all I got.

There's one thing I won't never do, and that is to keep a store bill, like a heap of 'em does. You get a book, and the plunder you fetch and all you buy is sot down in it. Some of 'em says it works mighty queer sometimes. Old Mr. Hinkson don't read nor write, and he done tried it. He can reckon figgers right smart, though, and he kept tally on a board right along, and you never see a man so beat out as he were when he come to settle. Mr. Sill put on them big spectacles folks allows he wears to make him look wise, and studied over his books. Mr. Hinkson went walkin' round the store, thinkin' what he'd buy with what were comin to him. He'd made a heap of swaps one time and another. At last Mr. Sill looked over his specs, smilin' – he's got right pleasant ways – and says, 'Well, Mr. Hinkson, you and me's nigher square than I allowed we was. You don't owe me but a nickel.'

My old man were in the store, 'long o' some others, settin' round the stove. He said Mr. Hinkson sot right down atop of a keg o' nails that were standing open, and just looked at Mr. Sill. He opened his mouth once or twice like he were goin' to sass, but he never said nary a word. After a bit he got up, and pulled a nickel out of his pocket and put it on the counter. 'I'll take my book, Mr. Sill,' he says. Mr. Sill got red in the face, but he didn't say nothin'. He just signed the book and give it back, and Mr.s Hinkson walked out of the store, and he ain't never done no tradin' there since.

'Tain't only the stores that does tradin' round here. 'Pears like a heap o' the neighbors raises more corn than they need to, else they wouldn't be tradin' it for whiskey like they do. That's what's keepin' a sight of 'em so poor and no-'count. When once you begin swappin' corn for whisky, you're gone. It's like goin' over a precipice. Them that's goin' down is always catchin' on to things and carryin' 'em along to the bottom. Ain't nobody as drinks but wants a heap o' t'others to keep 'em company. 'Pears like it's lonesome kind of work. That's what's ruinin' the boys. If they was left to theirselves, they wouldn't touch a drop of the blamed stuff. Poor Mis. Jenkins – her as lives across the Deep Gorge – is seein' a sight of worriment along of her men folks takin' to drink. They still's right under 'em. She can't stop 'em goin' there, nor totin off the corn crap, but she 'lows the Lord can; so she's took to callin' on Him. Folks says she follers 'em prayin', and she's prayin' for 'em nigh all the time. She's plum scared lest they die in their sins. She's always beggin' the Lord to save their souls. Her least boy's only fourteen; him she always called her baby. 'Pears like she can't give in to have him go to the bad place."

"Does that little boy drink whisky?"

"The neighbors says he's the worst of the lot, but maybe his mother's prayers'll save him yet. Just do look at them young 'uns of mine!" Mrs. Hapgood exclaimed as we drew near her house. "Don't they look like a lot of turkeys roostin' on the fence?"

They did indeed.

"Now watch 'em drap when they see it's me and a stranger."

Sure enough, they all dropped to cover as we drove up, but the oldest girl popped up her head to reply when her mother asked how long they had been "watchin' out" for her.

"Nigh about ever since you been gone," she answered, with a grin; "we-uns ain't had no dinner."

"Now just harken to that!" said the mother.

"Tired as I be, I got to go to cookin' victuals soon as I get home."

Chapter 7: Barter

She tried to be cross, but she couldn't help laughing with motherly pride at the ow of dirty faces now peeping through the fence. The last I saw of her as I drove off she was bartering painted candy for grimy kisses.

II

The day after my talk with Mrs. Hapgood, I walked over to the Black Rock to see the sunset across Deep Gorge.

The path led out upon the brink of a precipice, so steep and sheer that as I looked into the chasm below I drew back in alarm. Throwing myself upon the ground, the feeling of fear vanished, and I was soon lost in contemplation of the glorious scene.

The sun had already dipped to the tops of the higher mountains, and the valleys and coves in the gorge before me lay in purpling shadows. Miles to the south a black cloud overhung the mountains, the sun raying under it at many points. Gradually its lower edges grew ragged, and fringed in sudden showers to the earth, that tossed it back in rosy mists.

These cloud-fringes separate into forms like human figures in flowing drapery. Rocking and swaying, they rise into the higher air currents. Then, righting themselves, they form in procession, and leading towards the setting sun, one figure, more beautiful than the rest, moves with stately grace at their head. It was such a vision, and the illusion so perfect, that as the movements of a belated butterfly near by attracted my attention, I shuddered to find myself not being wafted on rosy clouds into opening gates of pearl, but dangerously near the edge of a precipice.

As I drew back, the butterfly spread his wings and floated over the chasm. Recalled to earth, my eye caught sight of a thin column of smoke curling up from the depths below, and out of the growing evening silence leaped harsh voices, as of men and boys carousing.

I knew then that down among the gathering shadow was one of the distilleries which work such ruin.

Presently figures began moving up the steep path of the opposite declivity. They were in shadow, but there was still light to betray the unsteady gait of the climbers, while the soft air carried but too distinctly the sound of their discordant voices.

At the top of the ridge a woman's form, whose attitude puzzled me, was outlined against the yellow sky. Suddenly I remembered what Mrs. Hapgood had told me of Mrs. Jenkins and her persistent prayers, and I knew that I was close to the tragedy of a human soul.

She rose from her knees, and turned toward the west, standing for an instant with clasped hands uplifted, evidently watching the floating and now fading cloud-shapes. Then her arms dropped like leaden weights. The next moment she stepped lightly forward to where the path emerged, calling out cheerfully, "That you, boys? Come to supper. The chores is all done, and I got somethin' good for you."

For reply I heard foolish laughter, but the youngest boy went up to his mother and kissed her.

"She's putting her prayers into execution," I said to myself: "she'll save them yet."

The glowing cloud-forms had vanished, but between her and me hovered the butterfly over the chasm.

The Course of True Love

"What with weddin's and baptizin's, I never see sich doin's," said Bina Yerkes, bouncing in upon me one day as I sat peacefully knitting.

"What's gone wrong with you, Bina?" I asked, laughing, as I caught sight of her flushed face.

She laughed, too. "Heaps," she replied. "It's them Jasper gals. They mostly always rile me up dredful. They come along apiece o' the way with me just now, and they're just bound they'll git baptized next month. Why couldn't they 'a' done it last time? That's what I want to know. It's just their blamed contrariness. They don't care how much work they make for me."

"For you!" I exclaimed, in astonishment. "What have you got to do with the Jasper girls joining the church, Bina?"

"My land! 'tain't their joinin' the church I care about," she returned; "it's the washin'."

She laughed at my puzzled look. "Yes, the washin'," she said. "Preacher Jenks lives nigh on to fifteen mile from here, and it's too fur for him to bring his baptizin' clothes along. He always stays 'long o' we-uns, and Pop favorin' him in size, he always borrows his clothes to baptize in. Of course I have 'em all to wash every time, and branch mud's mighty hard to wash out. The reason them Jasper gals didn't jine last time were that they's bound they'd wait 'til they could git white cotton gownds to be baptized in," said Bina, in disgust. "Why, they'll show the very print o' their figgers! 'Tain't 'spectable. Decent women folks always wears black wool gownds pinned down tight to their stockings. Even then, it makes you feel right queer to come up out o' the water with the fellers standin' on the bank sniggerin'.

Chapter 8: The Course of True Love

Shucks! I ain't got no use for no sich as them Jasper gals, nohow. Anyways, I sha'n't have to wash their old white gownds, so I don't care if they git 'em plum full o' branch mud.

I didn't come in to tell you about them, though. Their meetin' up with me sort o' upsot me. Mom says I ain't got no call to bother my head about 'em, nohow. I reckon she's about right. I come from the weddin'."

As she paused and seemed to expect me to express surprise, I put as much curiosity as I well could into the question, "What wedding?" I didn't want to spoil Bina's story, but I had already heard that a young couple among the summer boarders had decided to have a quiet wedding in the village church before leaving the mountain.

"Why, Miss Petersen's, of course," answered Bina. "Her and Mr. Sanders was married in the church this mornin'. I was lookin' to see you-uns there. Wasn't you invited?"

When I admitted that we were not, I saw that we immediately fell a notch in Bina's estimation.

"I were," she said, proudly. "Why, *everybody* were there! The Mahones and the Harts, and Mis' Pratt and her young 'uns, was all there. I got my invite 'count o' washin' for old Mis' Sanders all summer."

The bride's family had had a cottage part of the summer, and the Mahones had supplied them with chickens, and the Harts with fruit and vegetables. I believe the Pratts had sent flowers to dress the church.

"There were a big talk first-off," resumed Bina, "agin' their usin' the church for a weddin'. Some on 'em reckoned it weren't right to open it weekdays, nohow, lest it were for preachin', or maybe a funeral. Some on 'em's got mighty old-fashioned ideas. They allowed as such goin's on as weddin's wasn't religion. Mr. Sanders got right mad. He asked 'em what they done took him and Miss Petersen for, anyhow. He said if there were anythin' solemner or

71

more religious nor gettin' married, he'd thank 'em to tell him what it were. That settled it. He's a mighty nice young man. Him and her's took right smart interest in the Sunday-school this summer, and they didn't want to rile him.

He hired Uncle Lem to haul a sight o' spruce pine and laurel to trim up the church with. Uncle Lem allowed as it were a right smart waste o' money to spend it fixin' up the church the way they done just for one day, but Mom told him if they paid him well it weren't no concern o' his'n. He's own brother to Mom.

He laughed, and said she were most generally right, 'specially when she were ridin' her high horse. That always makes Mom mad," said Bina, with a laugh. "He means when she's tellin' you 'tain't none o' your business, nohow. She's right apt to say that when you're tellin' her things about other folks, and Uncle Lem likes to joke her about it.

He got paid all right, and you never see nothin' so pretty as the way the church were fixed. It were all green branches nigh the pulpit, with posies stuck in among 'em everywheres. And don't you think," said she, waxing enthusiastic, "right over where they stood when the preacher were a-marryin' 'em were a big thing – looked like a bell – made out of daisies and sich. It were all white."

"And what of the bride?" I asked.

"Well, she weren't much pretty to look at, but I wisht you could a' seen her gownd!" replied Bina. "It were all white silk, and dragged on the floor away behind her. They had to lay down things for her to walk over after all the folks was in. Her neck were all bare, though. It made me feel right queer, but some on 'em said they'd seen boarder ladies dressed that way before. They was pokin' fun at Uncle Lem. He was allowin', after we came out, that Miss Petersen's Ma put sich a sight o' stuff in the skirt o' her gownd that there weren't none left for the waist. Uncle Lem likes his joke.

Chapter 8: The Course of True Love

I see him lookin' mighty sharp at the bride, like as if he though that kind of a gownd right nice. It wouldn't do to tell Aunt Sally that," she added, laughing outright. "Old as they be, she's plum jealous o' Uncle Lem.

But I didn't finish tellin' you about the bride. She had a long white veil hangin' down her back that covered her up a little, and you never see sich gloves as she had on! They come way up her arms. T'other boarder young ladies, them as showed folks where to set, had on same kind. They had white shoes, too, and white dresses, and bunches o' flower in their hands. They looked right pretty.

Two young men was a-standin' by the door all the time. One of 'em took folks' tickets, and t'other kept sweepin' out the mud. It rained right smart last night. All the boarder folks come in carriages, but there were a sight o' mud."

I inquired if there was any music.

"Yes," was the reply; "a boarder lady done played a kind of dance tune on the organ for 'em to step to when they was comin' in and goin' out. I ain't right sure I liked that part in church."

"Why not Bina? Don't you think the Lord likes cheerful music?" I asked.

"Well, Preacher Smith allows as no music but psalm singin' ain't right nohow," she answered. "He can't abide the very name of dancin'."

"But they didn't dance at the wedding, did they?" I inquired.

"Not exactly," replied Bina, slowly; "but they done kept step to the music, and Preacher Smith allows as that's nigh about as bad as dancin'."

I asked if he was at the wedding.

"No, he weren't," Bina answered; "but he come along by our house one day when Bob were playin' on a mouth-organ, and Melindy were a-skippin' about keepin' time to the music. Lor'! she's

73

sich a little thing she ain't never heard tell o' dancin', and Mom was mighty vexed to think he seen her skippin' like that.

He done told Mom it were her duty as a professor to take that there mouth-organ away from Bob if he done played them dance tunes again. And he allowed as no church member were bringin' up a child the way it ought to go to let 'em hop and skip to music like Melindy were doin'. Mom, she cried, and Melindy run and hid."

"And what of Bob?" I asked, smiling, as I thought of his gaunt figure and expressionless face in connection with "dance music."

"Bob didn't say nothin' to the preacher," was Bina's reply. "After he were gone, though, he allowed as it were mighty queer if the Lord cared what tunes a feller like him played on a little old mouth-organ, and him earnin' the money to buy it, too."

I laughed, and Bina, emboldened, went on.

"And Bob said he reckoned the Lord knowed what he were about. Wasn't it Him as set all the young critters in the world a-skippin' and a-playin'? Bob said. "And who sot all the birds a-singin', I'd like to know, and even the trees a-makin' music every time the wind blows?" Bina asked, triumphantly.

"Bob says Melindy's only one o' the young critters, anyhow."

"I quite agree with him," said I, heartily. "I didn't know Bob was so sensible."

"Lor'! Bob's got a heap o' sense – real horse sense," answered Bina. "You wouldn't think it to look at him though." To which I gave inward assent, but as I said nothing, Bina continued:

"He's done played a sight o' dance tunes since then. He reckons if the Lord cares for music, He likes 'em a heap better'n sich dawdly old tunes as they puts up at preachin'. Bob ain't never got religion; he ain't even sot on the mourners' bench. He's a right good boy at home, though, and Melindy sets a heap o' store by him."

Chapter 8: The Course of True Love

Bina watched me silently while I picked up a dropped stitch in my knitting. Then she asked, smiling, "Did you hear tell o' Jake Ham's weddin'?"

"No; was it a fine one?"

"Not much fine," laughed Bina. "Jakes queer, anyways, and him and Viny Bangs had been courtin' more'n a year, and t'other day he allowed as they might as well get married. So they took hold of hands and started to find Mr. Spence – he's the justice, you know – to marry 'em. He weren't at home, and Mis' Spence told 'em he'd gone to the settlemint; so Jake and Viny followed him.

Me and the Bent girls was comin' along the road just as they come up with him. We-uns just said howdy, and went right on. As we was passin', we heard Jake tell Mr. Spence, no, they hadn't time to go along back to his house, 'cause it were nigh time to hunt the cows.

Then Mr. Spence hollered for we-uns to come back. 'I want you gals for witnesses,' says he; 'we're goin' to have a weddin'.'

Jake and Viny looked plum foolish standin' there in the road. We-uns wanted to laugh, but Mr. Spence pulled off his hat and went right on marryin' 'em. Jake's awful tall and thin, and he kept on his hat, and got all sort o' skeery. He kept crackin' the joints o' his fingers all the time. Viny's mighty little. She acted like she wanted to run away before Mr. Spence got through. They went off holdin' hands and smilin' for all they's worth, though. Mr. Spence and me and the Bent girls was all they was at that weddin', so you see it weren't much fine. Jake's cousin Lank Crane's been gettin' married, too."

"Why, he's nothing but a boy," I exclaimed.

"Lor'! that's nothin'," said Bina, with a broad grin. "He's done married the widder o' Bill Drayton, him as died a while back."

"She's almost old enough to be his mother," said I, indignantly; "and besides, she has a lot of children."

"Not now she ain't," Bina returned, significantly. "She done got her people to take 'em soon as ever Bill died. Bill's folks took two on 'em. They was right peart young uns, but she allowed as she couldn't do for 'em nohow. Bill weren't never no hand to git along, and they seen hard times, him and her. When he were gone, she said she'd lived on the floor o' the cupboard long enough, and now she were goin' up onto the shelves. So, she done put away the children, and swung a free foot. Then her and Lank went to courtin', and now they're married."

Bina got up and changed her seat. She was quiet a few moments, then she said, abruptly; "I don't guess you see that young man Mr. Black's got to run the sawmill? His name's Thompson, George Washington Thompson."

"What a fine-sounding name!" I said, by way of showing an interest in Bina's new theme.

"He's a mighty fine young man," she said, bridling. Glancing up from my knitting, I surprised her blushing.

"Now Bina," said I, "you're surely not going to fall in love with that young man after telling me you wouldn't leave home for the best man living?"

"I done done it," she answered, testily. "Him and me's sweethearts."

"Have you known him long, Bina?" I asked. She hesitated. "I ain't to say knowed *him* long," she replied, "but he's kin to the Mahones, and they allow as he's a right peart young man."

"So there's to be another wedding is there, Bina? Well I hope you'll be happy."

"No fear but what I'll be happy 'long o' him," she answered, with spirit. Then glancing at the clock, she jumped up, saying, "'Tain't that late, is it? I must be goin'. He allowed he'd quit work early today. I reckon he's waitin' by the branch for me now," she added, with a bright smile and heightened color. "Good evenin'. Come and see us," she said, and was off.

Meeting her a week later, I ventured to express the hope that the course of true love was running smoothly in her case.

"Oh, that's all fell through," said Bina, scornfully. "*He drinks*, and I wouldn't marry a gold man what drinks. I didn't care nothin' for him, nohow," she added, sharply, as she tossed into a laurel bush the bunch of wild flowers she had been twirling in her hands. "You can't trust no man," said Bina, doggedly, jerking leaves off the laurel bush and casting them from her as she spoke.

I was greatly surprised, but I only said, "So, there'll not be another wedding, after all, Bina?"

"No, sir!" she returned, emphatically; "not for him and me. He may go 'long where he come from, for all me. I ain't goin' to marry no such low-down, no-'count trash as him."

Chapter 9: Hiding Out

Hiding Out

"Marigolds is mighty pretty flowers, and powerful easy to raise," said Cinthy Ann, gathering a bunch of them for me while she talked. "They don't need no boxin', and horgs won't touch 'em 'count of their bad smell. Onct I had a dress the very color that there one in your hand; it were in war times. Nigh about all the men folks was hid out, and…"

"Hid out? What does that mean?" I interrupted.

"Why, you see we-uns hadn't nary niggers, and the men folks allowed as they hadn't no call to fight for 'em to please nobody; so they lit out and hid where nary side couldn't ketch 'em."

"But I don't see what that had to do with your yellow gown," said I, bewildered.

"Lor' me! that weren't nothing to what some of 'em had -- red and pink and sky-blue, so's you could see 'em a mile off."

"But what for?" I persisted

"So's they wouldn't shoot us for men folks. When they seen 'em, they done shot at the men what hid out like they was birds. My old man he done hid out. He were powerful fond of me and Jemimy-- that's her over in the lot hoeing corn; she were just a baby them times."

Looking in the direction indicated by Cinthy Ann, I saw a lank girl in a pink sunbonnet, resting on her hoe as she talked to a gawky youth leaning on the fence.

"Him and her's courtin'," said Cinthy Ann, with evident pride; "his Pa's mighty well-to-do."

"And is the young man himself steady and well-to-do?" I asked.

"'Bout like common," replied Cinthy Ann, "His Pa won't see 'em want if they git married."

I was getting used to this idea that young couples were to rely upon their parents, and I made no further comment, and Cinthy Ann returned to her story.

"Where was I at? Oh, yes; Jemimy were a baby, and Doniram--that's my old man; his Ma give him that name for a missionary the preacher heard tell about. Well, Doniram said nobody weren't going to git him to no war to leave we-un alone; so he done hid out. He crept round nights and fetched all the wood and water for me, and I done cooked all his victuals and put 'em in the spring-house, where he could get 'em handy. I weren't never no great cook, but he said I done made things real tasty them times. He kept us in fresh meat, snaring boomers and birds, and sich, and they was mighty good eatin'."

"Weren't you afraid he'd be caught by the soldiers?" I asked.

"Lor'! it weren't the soldiers we-uns was afraid of; it were them home guards, they called theirselves. They staid to home, they said, to see that other men done their duty goin' to war; and was mighty sharp after them as hid out. It were along of one of them that Doniram were nigh ketched onct."

"Tell me about it," said I, looking off over the peaceful landscape, and trying to imagine how it had seemed when the tragedy of war overshadowed it.

"One day," said Cinthy Ann, "one of them home guards come to the house; his name were Brown, and he lived over to the settlemint. None of the men what were hid out had got took, and Doniram were getting careless-like about being seen, and I allowed some one had told Mr. Brown he were nigh about home. He done axed me real polite where was Doniram. Done gone to the mill, I says, real peart, letting on like I reckoned Mr. Brown didn't know as he was hid out. He were a mighty sharp man, and there weren't much he didn't know, except that *I* knowed he'd joined the home guards. I done heard it that very morning. Mis' Plank done told me, when she come over to borrow some frivoles to make light bread. Her man were hid

Chapter 9: Hiding Out

out, and she had on a gown as pink as a peachblow, and a sunbonnet as green as a pea pod. She looked for all the world like a big hollyhock flower walking along upside down. I done told her so, and she just perked up her lips that vain. She needn't, though, for she weren't much to look at, but her gown were mighty pretty."

"But about Mr. Brown," said I, switching Cinthy Ann back upon the main track.

"'Been gone long?' says he, careless-like," she resumed. "'Lor' me!' I says, letting on like I were mad, 'it takes men folks a sight of time to go to mill. If Doniram would mind the baby, I'd go there and back while he's thinking about it. But the minute you ask a man to tend his own baby you'd think it weren't no kin to him. Doniram says he'd a heap rather go to the mill himself than mind this gal,' says I, laughing, and tossing her up.

'Daddy! daddy!' says she, clapping her hands and pointing her finger out of the door.

'Where at, honey?' says I, laughing again. 'I reckon daddy wants his supper if he's done come back that quick.' But I tell you my heart nigh about stood still, for, as I told you, Doniram was getting careless, and I allowed that like as not Jemimy had seen him when she hollered out. I weren't going to let on to Mr. Brown, though. he didn't rightly hear what she said first-off, but the second time she hollered, and while I were laughing at her, he jumped up so sudden that he upset his chair.

'Where at, Sissy?' says he; 'where's your Pa?'

'What's your hurry, Mr. Brown?' says I, letting on like I hadn't heard him; 'better set a while and have some supper along with we-uns when Doniram gets back. I'm going to have fresh horg meat and sweet 'taters.'

I knowed he were powerful fond of good victuals, and I'd have cooked everything I could get my hands on to throw him off the scent of Doniram.

"'Bleeged to you, Mis' Jones,' says he, 'but Mis' Brown's expecting me home to supper, and I reckon I'd better be going along.'

I 'lowed he had, too, but I didn't say so.

'Come and see us, Mis' Jones,' says he, and went away.

I peeked out of that there little window, and when I see he weren't going towards the settlemint I knowed he were hunting my old man. I daresn't go out while he were about, and every noise I heard made me jump. I kep' a tin pail mighty bright and shiny to hang out by the door when I knowed it were dangerous for Doniram to come nigh the house, and I hung that out now. It were getting along to early candlelight, and I kept thinking, 'Suppose he don't see it?' 'til it 'peared like I'd have to run out of doors and holler, or go plum crazy. My folks and Doniram's had lived nigh neighbors ever since we was little, and me and him had always set a heap of store by one another. He'd run and give me the first bite of the nicest apple he picked up when he were a boy, and it 'peared like his pockets was always full of chestnuts and teaberries when he come nigh me. If they sent one of us on an errand, there weren't no keeping of t'other one back. The folks had to give in to our going together or go theirselves. I were sort of skeery going through the woods, but Doniram always let on like he weren't afraid of nothing. But I have to laugh when I think of the day he got took down. We was walking along chawing apples; Doniram give his a fling, and grabbed my hand all trembly-like. 'Run, Cinthy Ann, run!' says he; 'it's a bear!'

I hadn't seen nothing, but I were that scared I never stopped running 'til we met up with old Mr. Sikes, stacking straw.

'What's your hurry?' says he; and when we done told him, he laughed fit to kill hisself. 'Look behind you,' says he. We hadn't dar'st to before. We felt different now we was close to Mr. Sikes, so we both turned round. Then we hollered out and grabbed Mr. Sikes by the legs.

Chapter 9: Hiding Out

'Look out, sonny! Don't upset me,' he says to Doniram. 'Ain't cut your wisdom teeth yet; better look again, so's you'll know your friends when you see 'em.'

Sure enough! there were Pa's old black sow trotting after us, watching for more apple cores. We felt might mean, and we wisht we dar'st ask Mr. Sikes not to tell, but we knowed he would, anyway, so we went off holding hands, and when we was alone, Doniram up and kissed me.

I were thinking of them old times, and I knowed the lights would go out for me if he got shot, but I didn't dar'st to cry, lest Mr. Brown might come back. I done all the chores I could think of, except chopping some light wood, but I knowed if Doniram heard me at that he'd come home sure, for he ain't like some men; I ain't never had to chop wood. The baby went to sleep, and I kept walking about doing little things, but I reckon I were only making believe do 'em, for my fists were that tight shut they was all bloody afterwards where my nails had gouged in, but I didn't take notice. 'Long towards midnight I heard Doniram whistle, and when he come creeping in through the shed-room, I cried and cried, and he cried, too, like as if we'd never stop. 'I were most took that time, little gal,' he says, 'and I must light out of this mighty quick.'

I done give him a warm snack, and he slipt out, and I never set eyes on him for a whole month. You see, he 'lowed nobody were about, and he wanted to see me and the baby so bad that he were coming right up to the door when Jemimy called out that time. He done caught sight of Mr. Brown's back, and quicker'n a wink he were off again."

Cinthy Ann laughed as she finished here story. "You see that hill?" she asked. "Well, Doniram just rolled down it like a log. It's a powerful slick hill, and when he got to the bottom he hid where no Mr. Brown couldn't find him. That's the time I got my yaller gown. One night Doniram says: 'Next week's your birthday, Cinthy Ann, and I were going to surprise you with something I bought off a peddler, but I reckon I'd better give it to you now, lest I'm drove sudden to hide out for good. I'll go get it.' When he come back he brung me a bundle, and I quick tore the paper off, and there was yards and yards of yaller print, the very color of marigolds. I jumped up and give him a kiss then I throwed the stuff around me to see how it would look.

'That's right, Cinthy Ann,' says he, 'make it into a gown; and if I have to stay hid out, wear it every time you go anywheres, so's I'll know it's you if I'm where I can sight you.' And that's what I done," said she. "Doniram said he could stand hiding out with t'other fellers so long as he got a sight of that yaller gown to hearten him up; but when he didn't see it, he allowed the sun were set for him that day. He were always powerful softhearted about me, and he ain't got over it yet."

Chapter 10
In Maria's Garden

In Maria's Garden

Maria was generally accepted as an old maid, but she had had in her youth what she herself called "a little accident," which somewhat set her apart from that class. It didn't seem to have affected her later morals, however, nor her standing with her neighbors. The child had lived long enough to leave her with well developed maternal instincts, which made her kindly to all children.

She lived alone on a little hillside farm that dipped sharply down into a fertile cove, planted with fruit, now in profitable bearing. The joy and solace of her life, however, was her flower garden.

"I'll tell you just how I came to take to a garden," she explained. "My little Jinny were powerful fond of posies. It were a sight to see her runnin' to pick every one she could get hold of. She were a mighty peart young one. Just to please her, I brung in roots of wild flowers and planted 'em where I knowed she'd see 'em the first minute they come out. That there big bunch of red lily roots were one of 'em, and so were that golden-rod and them wild asters. But, Lor' me! they done spread all over the place since, and I ain't never had the heart to thin 'em out. I pick a sight of 'em for the children goin by to school. I'm right fond of children, and I like to please 'em. Flowers is mighty like folks," she added, laughing; "if you give some on 'em a inch, they'll take a ell. And then the actions of some on 'em! I often laugh all to myself to see the ways of 'em. There's them white dahlias, now. Yes, they're plum pretty, but they're too biggotty for me. They put me in mind of what a boarder lady told me. She'd been about a sight, and she said some place where she were at – I ain't no scollard, and can't never recollect names – folks always gets married in the morning, and then they drive all round the settlemint in a fine open wagon for the bride to show off. She said she were all in white, sitting up that stiff, with a white veil, and a wreath of white flowers on her head, and a big bunch of 'em in her

Chapter 10: In Maria's Garden

hand. Poor folks like us-uns they was, she said, and there's a sight of mountings there, just like here.

Now, them white dahlias looks like them brides to me, and I don't love 'em like I do some other flowers. Sunflowers, too, has a way with 'em that folks is like. T'other day a boarder young lady and her sweetheart come in to buy some posies. You see, I make right smart money out of my garden in summer. Well that gal were the fondest I ever see of flowers. She kept running about every which way, smelling of this and calling him to look at that. I give her the scissors to cut her own posies. I didn't allow to run about that way myself. But it didn't make no difference to that young man where she were at; his head were always turned that way, like she were his sun. He had a yaller straw hat sot back on his head, and when I see it a-turning this way and that I says to myself, for all the world he's just like a big sunflower.

He says, was that all I charged for them lovely flowers? – them was his words – when he come to pay, and he give me a dime extra. Yes, lots of these here things is just herbs. Folks uses 'em for teas and sich. Some on 'em's right good to smell of, too. There ain't nary a time, except midwinter, when I can't find some sort of a posy in my garden.

Did you say weren't I lonesome in winter? Yes, I be sometimes, but I have a sight of work to do. I ain't one of the skeery kind, and the dogs is right good company. I do piece work for the neighbors. I put together three big quilts last winter, and quilted 'em, too. Then there's my loom. One time and another I do a sight of weaving, and it keeps a body busy choppin' enough wood to burn. I ain't got much time to be lonesome.

But I sot in to tell you how I come to have such a sight o' flowers. It were along o' the school teachers. First-off I only had wild things and marigolds and such. Down to Jones' Branch there's a mission school for girls. Right good ladies the teachers is, too, and they've been mighty kind to poor folks. I been going, off and on, to their women's prayer-meeting, so I got to know 'em right well. It don't hurt nobody to do a little extra prayin' now and then, and it does we-uns good to get out and meet the neighbors. Some of the men folks is down on them meetings, though. They allow as the women's getting too many new-fangled notions. What about, did you say? Why whisky for one thing. Women see a sight of sorrow over the drink, but ain't knowed how to set about to help theirselves. Another thing is about eddicating the children. Men folks allows that what were good enough for them's good enough for their children. A sight of 'em can't read and write, and they ain't got no use for schools for the children. They reckon they get all the eddication they need workin' the land and such. Taking the interest they do in the neighbors, the teachers allowed they'd offer some prizes for the best flower gardens. I ain't in the settlemint, so I weren't in it; but they knowed me, and when they had seeds or roots to give away, they give me some. That sot me to trying to beat 'em all, prize or no prize, and I done it. I reckon that were the best kind of a prize, for folks comes ever so far just to see my garden.

Yes, them's prize pansies, sure; but it takes a sight of work to keep 'em that way. If they're left to theirselves, they run out. A heap of folks is that way, too. I reckon that's what ails a sight of poor folks in these parts. There ain't nobody to take no interest in 'em, and they never go nowheres, and the children just grows up anyhow. I don't reckon as the Lord sets it agin' 'em as hasn't nary a chance, no more'n He does agin' pansies. Yes, I know folks says we-uns might do better, and so we might. But there's a heap ain't got no better sense, and so long as they don't know no better, it's clear they can't learn. If all your folks drink whisky, you're pretty nigh plum sure to come to it yourself. But, mind you, I ain't making excuses for bad actions. I'm only telling you what I see, and what I've learn't tending flowers.

A boarder gentleman showed me as there wouldn't be nary flowers if it weren't for the bees coming and going all day long. When I see 'em I allow the strangers coming and going all summer is

Chapter 10: In Maria's Garden

like the bees. Poor folks has a sight to learn, and a heap of it is bound to go agin' 'em. Look at that bumblebee caught in this here flower," added Maria, quietly releasing a bee from a snapdragon. "That flower ain't got sense enough to know its best friends; and a sight of folks is that way, too. A heap of 'em has moved off the mounting to get away from boarder folks. Some on 'em acts plum foolish about it. If their children's up to any devilment, they lay it on the boarders, when it's all their own contrariness. No, I can't rightly say as I'm fond of all kinds of flowers. Some on 'ems queer. I plant all the seeds and things folks gives me, but I don't set no store by some on 'em. Now, there's them new-fangled phloxes, all pints and jags. I ain't got no use for no sich. I'm right fond of marigolds, though, and I feel like I were hurt myself when the frost ketches 'em. Yes, you're right, the mountings is fine, but it don't seem like they's the same comfort to me that flowers is. I reckon I'd miss 'em if I was to go 'way off; leastways, folks says you do. My brother Abner went to Nebrasky; there weren't nary one of the children left but him and me. Ma'd had seven. He got a scollard to write back to Ma that he'd give a heap to see the mountings once more before he died. He had the chills bad out there, and they run him into kinsumption. Ma took on powerful when she heard he were bad off. She wanted Pa to sell the farm to git money for her to go to him, he wouldn't hear to it.

Mr. Walton, what paints picturs, come by the day Ma got the first letter tellin how he were pinin' for the mountings, and she asked him would he read it to her. When he got through, she sot pounding back and forth on that old chair on the doorstep, with her apron over her head, but he see'd she were cryin', and he were plum sorry for her. Next day he come in with a pictur he'd painted of the mountings, like they look from the high pasture lot. He asked Ma did she know what it were, and she allowed as it must be a dunce as wouldn't know his own mountings anywheres. Well, he said he done painted 'em on purpose for her to send to Abner. She bust right out cryin', she were so glad. He done told her he'd wrop it up and back it, for he reckoned she wouldn't know how. And he said wouldn't she like to send some flowers, too, that growed nigh the old house, so she give him a bunch of chiny pinks. It weren't much more'n a week when a letter come back sayin' as Abner were dead, but that it would have done Ma's heart good to see how happy that pictur and them flowers made him. They wasn't hardly ever out of his hands, the letter said, and they was in 'em when he died; so they put 'em in his coffin.

Ma weren't never the same after that, and she and Pa went nigh about the same time. They's buried over there where you see them purple asters so thick. My little Jinny's layin' alongside of 'em.

Ma sot a heap o'store by them chiny pinks. Her ma brung the root when her folks come to the mountings to live. Granny were plum biggotty. She were always telling how she weren't brung up to live like we-uns. Her man died before I were born. I reckon he weren't no-'count, nohow. He were always tradin' horses and stock, 'til he nigh about traded away everything Ma's folks had. Granny married him after she come up here. Ma told us he never said nary a word when she got goin' on about how she were brung up. He allowed, maybe, it were all so, just as she said. He weren't acquainted with her before she come up here. It made her right hard to live with, and I used to git plum tired hearing her brag of the things she had where she used to live, and I wished she'd stayed there. But Ma never give her no disrespect, and she felt right bad when she died. She planted some of them chiny pinks on her grave.

Yes, I'm a right good hand at raising sweet peas. I sell a sight of 'em to the boarders. There ain't nary flower 'pears so all alive to me as sweet peas. They ain't so like folks as they're like to the birds, though. A body takes queer notions about flowers, working so much among 'em as I do and bein' mostly alone. You can't never rightly tell what it is about a garden that works up your feelings. Just to look at it is the mornin' when the dew's on it. It puts me in mind of Bible talk about jewels and pearls. Even them big stiff hollyhocks has trimmin's on their leaves mornings.

Chapter 10: In Maria's Garden

I done sold a sight of roses this summer. I've got some mighty fine ones. They've quit bloomin' now, though. But there ain't nary one I set sich store by as the wild ones. All them bushes alongside o' that big rock, with the clematis a-featherin' all over it, is wild roses. It's just a sight when they're in bloom. 'Pears like the school children would go crazy over 'em. It goes agin' me to let 'em break the bushes, so I gather a heap of 'em every day and put 'em where they can help theirselves.

The neighbors think I'm plum foolish to let such truck as them big elders behind that rock stay on my place. It ain't only that my little Jinny were wild after elder-blows that makes me love 'em. I ain't sure I know just what 'tis. But, my Lor'! if you want to see something pretty, just come here when the wild roses is out and them elders standing up behind 'em hanging full of while blossoms. The least mite of wind sends 'em flying like feathers over that old brown rock. I take queer notions sometimes, like they was all playing together, with the birds joining in.

No, a body can't never tell what 'tis about a garden that works up their feelin's. I come out here one mornin' this very summer, when the dew were a-shinin' on them wild roses, and morning-glories was bustin' open everywheres, and elder-blows a-siftin' like snow all over that there rock, and before I knowed it I were settin' down in a heap cryin'!

Some of the boarder folks that come here has a mighty biggotty way of talkin', so I can't hardly tell what they're aimin' at; but I heard one that were lookin' over the fence at my garden t'other day say somethin' that kind o' stuck by me. I asked her to say it over again. It were 'a thing of beauty is joy forever.' I've studied over it a sight, and I reckon it hits that old rock complete. When the roses and other things is climbing all over it, you ain't no call to take note of much else. But when the frost ketches 'em, they're done for, and pretty soon there's nothing left but stems. Then it 'pears like the old rock laughs up into my face, for it's covered all over, where it ain't mossy, with the beautifullest red and green galax you ever see. Colt's foot, some calls it. It stays like that all winter. When the sun hits it on top, it's all shiny, and if you look through it, it's like lookin' through red winder curtains. I don't know why, but the snow never lies on that there rock, and it's a sight of company to me dark winter days, seein' it all bright, most like fire. Yes," she added, reflectively, "a body learns right smart from a garden, and it works off a sight of nerves."

Chapter 11
The Summer Is Ended

The Summer is Ended

A rainy autumn day was drawing to a close as, tired of indoor occupations, I started for a walk. All view was shut out by a heavy fog which swayed and lifted fitfully in the lessening gusts of wind, but gave no hint of blue sky or distant mountains beyond. It was a day to note the things underfoot and near by, rather than to lift one's eyes to the hills. The fast-bronzing galax, its lustrous leaves loaded with moisture, spreads like a jewelled tapestry upon the ground and rugged boulders by the roadside. The great brown lichens, turning up their olive-green edges in the dampness, as well as the lesser lichens and mosses - their neutral tints vivified by the rain - lend harmony to nature's beautiful handiwork, with which she so lavishly adorns her rough-hewn castles. The overhanging rhododendrons hold their slim green hands atilt, letting the moisture drip from their tips upon the galax below. Beneath lies a carpet of leaf-mold, giving off pungent odors as it soaks up the rain and sends the overflow trickling down every slant.

Above all droop the brown oaks, clutching fast their dying leaves, which they mean to flaunt through the winter in the face of ragging snowstorms, and to rattle like castanets in the teeth of the wind. The rain fills their brown hands, spilling over upon their neighbors. It is easy to imagine that you hear them all laughing together when swept by a gust of wind.

Except for the busy little snowbirds, there are no birds to be seen, and no sudden bursts of song enliven the way. Sometimes a frightened rabbit or chattering squirrel darts across the road, or a long-legged pig dashes into the bushes at sight of me; but of human interest there is none.

Suddenly, at a turn in the road, I heard quick, splashing footsteps behind me and a child's laugh. I turned to give greeting to my fellow-traveller through the fog, and looked into one of the saddest

Chapter 11: The Summer is Ended

faces I had ever seen. It was that of a young woman, a mere girl I thought her, carrying a child. She was miserably clad for such a day, and the baby's feet were thrust out bare from under the old shawl which she held over the child and herself. She stopped beside me to shift the child and a basket she carried to opposite arms.

I asked if she was tired.

"Yes, marm," she replied; "I'm mighty tired. I've been up to the settlemint scouring for Mis' Hall; I reckon you know her. She gives me work once a week, and some cold pieces to take home; that's what's in my basket."

"Are you a widow?" I asked.

Her face darkened and flushed. "No, I ain't no widow. I wisht I was," she added bitterly. "I ain't never been married. I met with a accident."

"You have a dear little baby," I said.

"Yes, she's all the comfort I got. Folks done turned against me when they found she were comin'. I tried to drown myself, I were that miserable, and I tried to git rid of her, too, poor lamb!" she said, hugging the child closer. "You wouldn't think it to look at me now, but I were a right pretty gal, and chockfull of fun and devilment. I never meant no harm, though. I run about a sight, and had lots of sweethearts, but I held my head high, 'cause my folks was mighty well-to-do, and I wouldn't look at no feller to marry him. Granny used to say I'd go through the woods and pick up a crooked stick at last. I done it. When Jason Briggs, that all the gals was set on catchin', come after me, he turned my head. He could talk that slick you'd believe every work he said, and think you was goin' straight to heaven along with him. Many's the time I've watched a big pink cloud when the sun were settin', and felt like him and me was floatin' away on it.

He asked me to marry him first-off. He said I were the only gal he ever see that he wanted to marry. He talked like all the rest of the gals wasn't nowhere alongside of me, and I believed him. But he said his folks was plum set against him marryin' at all, so we must keep quiet 'til his Pa died. The doctors allowed he were like to die any minute of heart complaint, so Jason said. The old man's living yet," said the girl, with a forced laugh.

"Jason talked like his own folks used him hard. He allowed if it weren't for me bein' so good to him and lovin' him so well, he couldn't stand it nohow, and he'd quit and go away off West. Some days he talked like he were goin', anyway, 'til I'd get plum wild listenin' to him. I axed him if he were so sot on goin' why couldn't him and me marry, and me go along; but he always had some good excuse that I swallowed like it were gospel truth.

I ain't the only gal that's went wrong, and I needn't tell you the rest; but when a gal forgets to hold herself dear, she may be plum sure the man holds her cheap. That's how it were with me and Jason. When he found he'd got me into trouble, he quit comin' nigh me, and the next I knowed, he'd gone way off, sure enough. Then I took to crying and crying night and day, and my folks suspicioned what was the matter, and turned me off. I'd have been in a bad fix, if it weren't for Ma's aunt, old Miss Johnson. She were a right good old woman, but she were gettin' puny, and she allowed I'd be a sight of company if I'd stay with her. Lord knows, I were glad of a place to go to, and I done helped her all I could with the work. She were mighty good and kind to me, and I can't never forget it. She's dead now. 'Pears like she knowed the world had all gone black for me, and when she see me cryin' or goin' off towards the dam, she'd say somethin' kind, or she'd reckon she'd take a walk, too, and she were glad she needn't go alone. Then she'd think of good things out o' the Bible to tell me, or maybe out of a book she had called Pilgrim's Progress. She were a good reader – better'n me, for I were all for havin' a good time when I went to school. She weren't no hand to preach nor to scold a body that's down, but she knowed how to get your mind off your troubles. I didn't know then that she'd had a

Chapter 11: The Summer is Ended

dreadful trouble herself when she were young. It weren't like mine, though, she were too good a woman for that.

When the baby come, she made a sight of fuss over it. I hated the poor little thing first-off, but I couldn't keep on doin' it with a good woman like her lovin' it so. She'd talk to it like it were to be a great holp and comfort to its Mammy, and grow up a good girl that no man couldn't ruin. I knowed she were only talkin' for me to hear, and when I see she were failin' fast I began to pay heed to all she said. It's all along of her that I've tried to live right, and take care of my baby. She died when Maggie were four months old," said the girl, bursting into tears; "and it's the Lord's truth that I ain't got nary a real friend in the world since. My people live over to Beech Farms, and they ain't never give no sign for me to come back home. I'm sort of scared for Maggie to go among 'em, anyway, for fear they'd throw up agin' her what she couldn't help. Aunty Johnson left me her little place, but it took all the money she had for her sickness and buryin'. Her and me workin' together couldn't make enough out of the old place to keep us in victuals, and I ain't much strong any more to work in craps, no how. Some of Aunty's folks out West sent her money twice a year. That's how she got along. I'd be glad to get more work to do, but some folks lets on like it would hurt 'em to have such as me around, and most don't want to be pestered with a baby. You can't blame 'em, for babies is a sight o' trouble."

"Would none of your neighbors look after her?"

"I could leave her with old Mis' Peters now she can walk and talk, for she allowed she'd take care of her if I'd give her half I earned. But they do say she were right cruel to her own young 'uns, and nobody sha'n't abuse you, shall they, honey?" she said to the child, giving it a motherly hug.

"Most of them as has sons," she resumed, "is afraid to have me comin' to their houses to work, but they needn't be. I've had enough of men. I wouldn't look at the best one ever lived. No, nor I wouldn't believe he meant honest by me, not even if we was standin' up before a preacher to be married," she added with a hard tone.

We had been splashing along through the mud while she was talking, the baby playing bo-peep with me, or patting and kissing it's mother's face.

"She's a peart one, ain't she?" said the girl, as the baby clapped its hands and said "moo!" to a cow by the roadside. "It's mighty queer sometimes to think she won't never have no father to see her pretty ways, or for me to tell about her new tricks when he come home. It would be that way if I was a widder woman, I reckon. Only then I'd be thinkin' how he'd love her, and that maybe he seen her and me now, though we couldn't see him. But now my heart's all black and bitter whenever I think about Jason. He were the only one I ever loved, you see, and that makes it worser. Aunty done told me I must try to forgive him. Maybe I could if I never see him, or heard tell of him. Mis' Hall done told me this mornin' he were back again, and courtin' one of the Brown gals. Nice gals they be, too. When I come up with you I were thinkin' I could kill him if I wasn't a coward and afraid I'd get hung. It's a chance if I don't do it yet. My heart seems to me them times like one o' them black hog-wallers. 'Pears like I were sinkin' in the black mud and couldn't get out. Then, maybe, Maggie does somethin' pretty and cute, and makes me laugh, and I feel like I were walkin' on God's earth again. But I can't never tell when I'll be flounderin' in the waller again. It scares me to think how easy a body might do a murder them times. Sometimes I think I ought to see Jason and warn him to keep clear of me, and then I'm afraid I might do it right then and there. I've studied about it a sight, and I don't know what I'd ought to do. It's hard lines for the girl to have all of the cruel sufferin', and be looked down on by everybody, and the man go free. 'Pears like he ain't no worse thought of, and he can marry most any nice girl he wants. I don't know why I've told you all this," said the girl, the tears streaming down her cheeks, which the baby was softly stroking as she snuggled closer to her mother, cooing, "Pitty mammy, don't ee cry."

Chapter 11: The Summer is Ended

"I ain't talked like that to a livin' soul since Aunty died, and she's been gone more'n a year. I feel like everybody's hand were agin' me, and maybe that makes me more biggotty. It's easy keepin' 'count of them as has took notice to her or me since the baby come. The new doctor were plum kind to me when she were sick last summer. I done took her to his office once, and she taken to him right off, and put out her tongue so pretty when he said to that he gave her a pictur to carry home. A body can't forget them that's kind to 'em when they're down."

I had been holding my umbrella over her as we walked, but we were both getting very wet, and it was time for me to turning homeward.

"Have you much farther to go?" I asked, not liking to leave her unsheltered in the rain.

"No; that old cabin down in the holler is where I live. Right here's the bars I go through. I'd be plum glad if you'd come to see me sometime when you're passing," she added, wistfully. "I know nice folks don't like the name of visiting such as me, though."

Promising to stop for a rest the next time I came by, I turned to go. Then I remembered that I did not know her name.

"It's Debby Cooper," she said, in reply to my inquiry. "The baby's called after Aunty; her name were Margaret, and I call the baby Maggie. Good evenin'. I wish you well. It's been a sight o' help to have somebody to talk to."

As I walked briskly toward home, trying to shake off the chill of the dampness, which seemed to strike through me, I no longer saw the wondrous tapestry effect, nor any of Nature's marvels, which had so beguiled me outward bound. The world that lay about me seemed wrapped in deadly shades.

A White Day

I

Silently throughout the damp winter night the hoarfrost has been at work. Dawn finds a thick rime upon every lichen that decks the bare trees, every laurel leaf, every mossy stone, the bronzed leaves of the galax that carpets the ground, and upon the very ground itself.

A white world flashed into radiance when the sun rose. Sudden mists veiled his face ere he could undo the frostwork of the night, and then followed one of those wondrous "white days," seldom seen but among the mountains.

Gleaming and sparkling in the hazy light, the frosty air spreads its white net, and with silent witchery all things are transformed.

While out for a walk, we laugh to see one another grown suddenly gray, and hand-in-hand, like two children, find interest in trifles. The clouds of steam rising from the plodding oxen and falling again in snowy shower upon their rough coats, as well as the clumsy puppy fighting frost from his face, offer diversion to our light mood. We amuse ourselves guessing the identity of nebulous human forms in frosty draperies. At sight of a girl with powdered hair and gleaming garments, haloed with mist, walking beside a youth thrust into sudden dignity by whitened hair and frost toga, our imaginations take fire.

We behold in them the embodiment of perpetual youth, with its old, old story, and our handclasp tightens as they draw near. We surprise the young lovers, for such they are, by the warmth of our greeting.

We, too, have dreamed dreams, and memory is busy with the time when we began to walk the long path together, our world palpitating in glowing white.

The girl was Bella Comly, who, having been to the school at Hinkson's Corner, spoke better English and appeared better in consequence. Some sewing she was doing for me gave us an excuse to stop and talk with her a few moments.

Having heard of her engagement to Harry Heath, who was her escort, we had some curiosity to meet him. He seemed a good fellow, and they both looked very happy.

Bella said she was coming to see me in an hour for further directions about the sewing, so after exchanging a few commonplaces, we parted.

When she called, the matter of the sewing was soon dispatched, but I saw from her manner that she had another errand, which she found hard to broach. It came out at last when I spoke of the beauty of the white day. She exclaimed, with a blush: "It's a white day for Harry and me, and I want you to know about it. When you met us on the road, we had just been to 'Squire Brown's to get married."

Laughing at my astonishment, Bella continued: "I'll tell you how it was. You know Harry and I both went to Hinkson's to school, his folks live over there. They're not so well-to-do as my people, and my father's been plum set against my marrying one of that stock, as he calls it. No matter what good he heard of Harry, he'd up and say, 'The stock's there.' Father's right stubborn, and I favor him in that. The more he talked against Harry, the more set I was on having him. Father allowed there wasn't one of Harry's folks that had ever amounted to shucks, and he wouldn't hear to it that Harry was different. He is, though. He paid his own way at school, and he's got the farm he's buying near us part paid for. He owns a yoke of steers and a wagon and a cow, and he has 'em all paid for.

Chapter 12: A White Day

There wasn't a better boy in school than Harry; the teachers will all tell you that. He and I were sweethearts from the start. Neither of us ever wanted to look at anybody else, so it wasn't much use trying to part us. Mother wasn't so set against him as father was. She couldn't bear to see me feeling bad, so she's been sort of encouraging us when father wasn't by. That heartened Harry to go on getting things and fixing up his place like we expected to marry; but father wouldn't give in to it. Harry wanted me to go off and get married anyway. He said father'd come round all right when he found he couldn't help himself. Maybe he would have, but it seemed like I couldn't treat father that way. Harry's folks are different. He hasn't any call to go out of his way to please 'em; but father's always been good to me, except about this, and I couldn't go back on him like that.

Well, Harry got mad at last, and said I didn't love him. He declared he'd sell out and go West; he meant it, too. That's three weeks ago. He said he'd give me just a month to decide. I told mother, and she talked to father; but he got angry, and said: 'I wish he would go West; I'll buy his place myself to get shut of him.'

Mother allowed he'd never give in now. It made me plum sick; I couldn't sleep, and I cried every time I thought how awful it would be when Harry was gone and I'd have to go by his place and see strangers there. I couldn't eat, and I couldn't read or sew, or feel any interest in anything, and poor mother did nothing but study about me. The house was like a funeral, but father appeared like he didn't care.

Then Jenny Anson, who was at Hinkson's when I was, got worse. You know she died of the fever yesterday. Mother was over there a good deal, helping Mrs. Anson, and when she'd come home she'd tell how Jenny was like to die, and how bad her folks felt. Yesterday she came back when father and I were eating breakfast, and threw herself into a chair by the fire, and cried and cried, so she could hardly tell us Jenny was dead.

Father was scared at first, for mother ain't one of the crying kind of women. He just smoothed her hair without saying a word, but the tears were running down his cheeks. Then he went out to tend the cattle, and mother and I sat there crying. I wasn't crying about Jenny, though; I was crying about Harry and me, and wishing I was dead like Jenny.

The neighbors came hurrying along to see Mrs. Anson as soon as they heard Jenny was dead, and everybody had something to say to father out there in the yard about how awful it was for the Ansons to lose their only girl. Toward night Harry came by with his team. When I heard his whistle, I went out to speak to him. I was in hopes he had come round, and was going to tell me he wouldn't sell out and go West if father held out. Mother saw us, and told father he'd better give in for us to marry, for, like as not, I'd go the way Jenny did. She allowed there wasn't anybody so peaked as I was then that could stand up against anything. Folks do say Jenny was crossed in love, and that was why she'd got so puny that she hadn't any chance against the fever.

Father studied a while. Then he said: 'Mother, I know you're right, but I've stood out so long that it comes mighty hard for me to give in for all the neighbors to make talk about. You can go out this minute, though, and tell those children I give my consent, provided they'll go off and get married without saying anything to anybody and not tell you or me, either.'

I was feeling pretty bad just then, for what Harry came to tell me was that Mr. Bagley had made him an offer for his team and his cow, and said he must decide about it in three days. Harry felt bad, too. He hadn't even got out of the wagon to talk to me.

When mother came out and told us, 'You don't mean it, Mother Comly!' he says, and jumped right out and whirled me round like we were dancing. Then we ran into the house and hugged and kissed father 'til he put his head down on the table and cried like a baby.

Chapter 12: A White Day

Mother didn't cry, though. She just laughed, and told Harry to hitch his team to the fence and stay to supper, and she said for me to fly round and get it ready, if I knew whether I was on my head or my heels.

I got my appetite back that minute, and I put so much on the table the folks poked fun at me, for I was too flustered to eat, after all. When I went out with Harry to bid him good night, he said: 'Get your things together, little girl, for I'm going to move you into your own house to-morrow.' That took my breath away, and I hid my face against his coat and said it was too soon. Harry only laughed when he kissed me, and said for me to meet him at the turn of the branch this morning at nine o'clock. He said he'd fix it all right so's we'd be sure to find 'Squire Brown at home.

Father was out of the way when I started, but I think mother mistrusted, for I saw tears in her eyes, though she let on to laugh, and said what a pretty white day it was. When I met up with Harry, both of us were white with frost. He said we looked like we were in bridal array, sure enough. He made me stop and listen to the waterfall by the turn of the branch, because he thought it sounded like bells. That was when the sun most shone out and everything looked pinky white. Harry said he didn't know the world could be so beautiful. We were so happy coming along that we laughed at everything and nothing, and we just loved the white day for coming for our wedding.

It didn't take 'Squire Brown long to tie the knot, as he called it. Mrs. Brown and Sara were witnesses.

When we first caught sight of you we were walking arm in arm, but we felt shy of your seeing us, so we let go. Then we saw you holding hands and not minding us, and wished we hadn't been so silly. But how I have run on," said she, rising; "I promised Harry I'd meet him at the store. We need some oil and flour and things, and he's gone to get his team. After we do our store errands, he's going to take me home to see the folks and get my things, and then we're going to our own house," Bella said, blushing. "When I get the place tidied up, I want you should come and see me. Good by."

The white day held its own to the end. Toward night the mists, sinking into the valleys below us, spread out into a billowy white sea that glowed rose-tinted at sunset. Like islands the mountain-peaks stand out of it, glinting in the last rays of the setting sun.

We, two, who still dream dreams, watch the scene as the rosy glow changes to the dull grays and deep purple shades of twilight, talking the while of other white days of long ago, 'til daylight fades.

Then darkness gathers, and there is no light but the light of stars.

II

"Now came still evening on, and the twilight gray

Had in her sober livery all things clad."

One fine spring day, when nature was smiling into leaf and bud, we went for a long drive, Karl and I, taking our lunch with us, and coming home by way of Edgely.

Whole families are abroad, clearing the land, and the smoke of burning brush veils the landscape. Everywhere rings upon the air the stroke of the ax, and we hear on all sides the thud of falling trees. Girdled long ago, they stand like grim specters awaiting their doom.

Ground squirrels dart across the road and eye us from fresh coverts in the briar-grown fences. Mountain boomers, playing a furtive bo-peep as they dodge around tree-trunks, chatter wildly at the sound of falling trees, while nesting birds vent their alarm in noisy restlessness.

Chapter 12: A White Day

Above the fragrant sassafras, the swamp maples swing their red tassels in the light breeze. Stiffly beside them stand the bare oaks, awaiting their spring robes of pale pink velvet. At their feet now lie the rustling brown garments that defied the winter and struggling through that dusky matting, the tender green of new galax is crowding aside the searing red and bronze of its old foliage.

Over all things spreads the spring magic, into whose net we too are swiftly drawn. All things are become new. There is no time, no death, nothing but youth with its old, old story. It is not we two who shall be no more when other springs shall ripple upon the shores of time. We are part and parcel of this ever-recurring miracle.

Toward noon the stony road, winding downward through dense rhododendrons, brings us to a stream that is hardly whispering as it runs away to the sea; yet far above its bed the telltale banks shout tidings of a recent destructive freshet; while on the brink the alders, in fringed weeds bestowed by the flood, mourn the ruin of their spring costumes.

We camped near the water, building our fire among stones that but the other day formed the bed of a rushing torrent. The horse munching his corn near by, and the startled sheep thrusting their heads out of the undergrowth, watching us askance, ready for flight, added to the charm of the peaceful scene. It was not peaceful long, however. When the razor-backed hogs in the surrounding wood smelled our hot lunch, the clan charged upon us, putting to flight our peace of mind, and the timid sheep as well.

We defended our rock table in the sneaking hope that the next freshet might bear on its bosom these same razor-backs in its mad rush through mountain gorges.

On our way home we found ourselves in the neighborhood of the Heaths, who lived on the Edgely road. We had not seen them since the "white day" of their marriage in early December, so we decided to call upon them. We found them at work in their garden; and it was a happy pair of faces that looked up to welcome us.

Harry tied our horse, and took Karl off to inspect the stock and talk politics, while Bella and I went toward the house. We stopped on the way to watch the young shepherd dog giving wild chase to the chickens.

"It's lucky for Pete the bees haven't got the spring fever like folks," Bella said, as the dog dashed in and out among the beehives. "Good old fellow, I love him because he's so fond of Harry." Rushing up to her at this moment, Pete, on hearing his master's name, gave her hand a hasty lick and bounded off in search of him.

Bella laughed happily when she saw him go, and we went on to the house. It was simply furnished, but was very neat, and had an unusual air of comfort.

After displaying with evident pride her pretty patchwork quilts and home-made devices for the adornment of her house, Bella, with flushing cheeks, confided to me the new hope just springing into life in their hearts.

"I'm so glad you came," said she, "for I want somebody to advise me. This makes me feel mighty young and ignorant, but I'm so happy, and I want to do what is right about taking care of myself. Harry's so glad. I thought he was as happy as a man could be before, but he's like a boy over this. He wants me to pick out names for a girl and a boy out of the Bible the teachers gave us when we were married. When I asked why our names wouldn't do, he said there couldn't be but one Bella in the world for him, and," added Bella, smiling, "I reckon I feel the same way about his name. There ain't many girls that have such a good husband as I've got. I haven't never had to carry water or fetch in wood, and Harry's more contented at home than anywhere. Father and mother have come to like him mighty well, too. Mother says they're right sorry they were so set against our marrying."

Later, seeing me look at the books on the shelf, Bella said, "Harry's a right good scholar. He reads aloud to me evenings while I

Chapter 12: A White Day

knit or sew. Sometimes we get down our school-books and hear one another the old lessons; it's a heap of fun."

Our "men folks" came in just then, Harry bringing eggs in his hat, and laughing about our encounter with the razor-backs, of which Karl was telling him. "But" said he, "I reckon I've got something to say about your wanting 'em carried off by the next fresh, for they're my hogs!" At which Bella laughed merrily. Happy, care-free souls; they bubbled into laughter at trifles, and walked with glad, springing steps, good to see.

When we were leaving, we found the fresh eggs bestowed in our lunch-basket. Harry, in reply to our protest, said, laughing, "That's to pay for the way our hogs pestered you."

There were many happenings to prevent our seeing the Heaths for a long time, but what we heard of them convinced us their "white day" held its own.

When the doctor told us of the arrival of Bella's baby girl, he confided to us the touching story of Bella lying exhausted after the baby came, while Harry, beside himself with alarm, kept kissing her pale face and limp hands, imploring her not to die and leave him. Anxious to give Bella the rest she needed, the doctor finally sent him from the room. Harry staggered into the next room, where the sturdy baby was yelling itself into the color of a boiled lobster. He dropped into a chair, taking no notice of the child, much to the disgust of the old women assisting at its toilet. There he stayed until the doctor told him he might see Bella again for a few moments. The loving smile with which she greeted him relieved his great anxiety. He told the doctor afterward that he could hardly keep from laughing when she asked him if the baby wasn't a beauty. He had quite forgotten to look at it, but was wise enough not to tell Bella so. She made a rapid recovery.

The baby was named Bera, because they found in the Concordance of their Bible that the name meant gift. Bella said they felt that the child had come to them as a blessed gift from heaven.

Three years passed, and just after the birth of their second child, Harry took the grippe, and was for a time very ill. His convalescence was very slow. Every attempt he made during the winter to resume his outdoor duties resulted in a relapse. This brought much anxiety and extra work upon Bella, who was by no means strong herself at this time.

Troubles seemed to thicken about them. Their cow wandered away in a snowstorm, and was found dead in a ravine, and some of their razor-backed hogs actually met the fate we had invoked for their progenitors.

I went one day in the spring to see Bella, and found poor Harry, wan and weak, alone with the babies. He said Bella had just gone on an errand to her mother's. As I was on horseback, and glad of an excuse for a longer ride, I decided to follow her. When I overtook her, Pete, the dog, was walking dejectedly beside her, while Bella's eyes were red with weeping, which broke forth afresh at sight of me.

I dismounted and tied my horse, and Bella and I seated ourselves upon a log in the woods. Pete, edging close to her, nosed Bella's face and hands, giving vent to his sympathy in whines and sniffs when her sorrow overpowered her. Having just seen Harry, it was easy for me to understand the wild burst of grief that shook the young wife, and I could not restrain my own tears as I sat beside her.

At last she spoke. "I hadn't any real errand to mother's. I just made up one, so I could get away alone to cry," she said. "My heart has felt all day like it were bursting, and I couldn't let Harry know. He spit blood this morning, a good deal of it, and I know, by the questions the doctor asked me when he came, that it means he can't get well. Harry's got so downhearted about himself that I have to keep up. He just clings to me like a child, but the Lord knows my heart's broken and my courage gone."

She wept bitterly for a while. Then she said, "We've been so happy; nobody knows like I do what a good, kind man Harry is. I

Chapter 12: A White Day

can't live without him, I can't, I *can't*," she cried, throwing her arms above her head and sobbing violently.

I sat dim-eyed looking at the mountains, while Bella's head sank lower 'til it rested upon that of the faithful dog. When her sobs ceased, I thought her asleep from exhaustion. Save for the sighing of the breeze in the old spruce pine overhead, or the rustle of a wood robin among decaying leaves, a deep silence lay about us. The echoes of more distant sounds failed to touch consciousness, though memory might blare them forth later.

Presently Bella raised her head wearily. "You see it's this way with me," she said; "I'm mighty easy disheartened when things go wrong. I take all the blame to myself, and get to crying sometimes like I'd never stop. Then Harry comforts me. He talks like I made his whole world, and couldn't do anything very bad anyhow. Before I know it he has me laughing at some of his jokes, and I think what a fool I've been, and I love him better than ever. But oh, my God! how shall I live without him?"

The shadow of a passing cloud suddenly darkened the woods. Bella threw back her head, crying, "Oh, it will be like that when Harry's gone, all dark. How can I bear it?" The cloud passed, and again the dancing sunbeams played about us, but she was unconscious of the change.

"The worst of it is," she said, after a while, "I don't feel to care anything for the children, especially the baby; they just seem to be taking my time away from Harry. I'm afraid I shall hate the poor little things when he's gone."

Alas! the "white day" was drawing to a close for poor Bella.

After she became quiet, I went on with her to her mother's, and then back to her own door. She had bathed her eyes at a spring, and resumed her usual manner, but she surprised me by the cheerful greeting she gave Harry. "Look," she cried out, laughingly, to me, as we drew near the house, "I do believe Harry and Bera have been

111

sitting in that doorway ever since I started, just waiting for me to come home." Harry laughed, too, and little Bera danced for joy in the light of her mother's cheerful presence.

"Mother sent you this fresh buttermilk, Harry; it will do you a sight of good," I heard Bella say.

As I rode off, Harry was smiling up at her as she poured the milk into a glass, while Pete, overjoyed to see them so cheerful, was jeopardizing the buttermilk by his antics.

It was the last time I saw poor Harry.

The twilight of their "white day" was a short one. Ere Bella's eyes had become accustomed to its somber hues, swift darkness gathered; the "white day" had joined the memory throng, and she was alone, with no light save the light of stars.

Chapter 13
Now is the Winter of Our Discontent

Now is the Winter of Our Discontent

I

Winter was coming on apace. Already the nights were cold, and hard frosts had shriveled and blackened, as with fire, every tender growing thing. The rough chestnut-burrs had opened and fallen at the touch of the north wind. The squirrels and bluejays had had out their quarrel over the nuts, and the jays had flown away southward, leaving the squirrels in peace with their winter hoard.

The oaks held fast their dry brown leaves, that rustled with every breath of air, but their crop of acorns was scattered on the hillsides, and the fattening hogs left long zigzag furrows among the dead leaves in their search for mast.

Every gust of wind sent the fallen leaves whirling far and wide in mad disorder. They banked at every obstacle, like drifting snow, and one must wade knee-deep through them at every turn. There was ice along the edges of the leaping mountain stream, while the rising sun surprised a rime of hoar frost upon the mossy trunks and limbs of the trees these mornings. As it beaded in the sun's warmth, the woods glinted, as with the sudden flash of jewels.

It was a time to look well to the winter's supply of food and fuel. We, with the prudence born of experience, had done so, but many of our neighbors were still trusting to luck to save them from the inevitable. They depended largely upon their crops of cabbages, potatoes, and apples for their living, and as there were no cellars to the houses, these must be buried before a hard freeze destroyed them. In the mean time they were heaped in the fields, and we could always feel sure that when the winter, after repeated warnings of his approach, gave us a final grip, he would still come unawares upon the improvident.

Chapter 13: Now is the Winter of Our Discontent

Mrs. Hansley came in on an errand one cold day, and had much to tell of the damage done by the heavy frost of the previous night. " 'Pears like some on 'em would learn not to git ketched this late with their cabbages and 'taters not buried, and their apples out, too," said she; "but it's that way every winter. Folks is so unthoughted. They'll work the whole summer making a crap o' cabbages, and then lose 'em all by freezin'. They can't never believe winter's comin' 'til everything they've got is froze stiff. Old Mr. Moss were runnin' 'round everywheres this mornin' tryin' to git somebody to help him bury his cabbages and 'taters, but the neighbors is all plum busy with their own craps. Yesterday he were runnin' about all the evenin' tryin' to borrow a bushel basket to tote his 'taters in. 'Pears like him and his old woman might a' toted 'em in buckets and got 'em all kivered in before night if he'd staid to home and sot to work at 'em. It were nigh dark when he come back without ary basket.

A sight of 'em loaded up their wagons yesterday to haul their cabbages and apples to Hinkson's to sell. If they hadn't 'em well kivered in, they're plum froze this mornin'. I see 'em all goin' down the road a while back, so I reckon they allow they'll git to sell 'em anyway. Mis' Cooper told me, as I come along, that she done her best to git her old man to put more hay and straw in the wagon to keep things from freezin', but he allowed it weren't worth while to haul a bite more'n the critters would eat whilst he's gone. He ain't forehanded like her. Like as not his things is all froze in his wagon."

I asked what he would do in that case, if he failed to sell them.

"Throw 'em all out," Mrs. Hansley replied. "It wouldn't pay to haul 'em back up the mounting. A heap of 'em has it to do. If it comes off steady cold, the neighbors'll have to help old Mr. Moss cut some wood. He ain't got nary a stick put up. I see him and Mis' Moss gatherin' brush in the woods nigh his house every mornin'. It takes a sight o' time to git enough for a fire, and it don't last no time, nohow. Most folks reckon he might 'a' chopped what wood he needed this summer, when he weren't doin' nothin' but settin' round the stores and chawin' tobacco."

"Then who does the field work?" I said.

"She mostly works the crap," said Mrs. Hansley. "They aint' made nigh enough corn to see 'em through the winter, and I see 'em t'other day feedin' of it out to their hens as has quit layin'. Their old cow's gone plum dry, and they'll have her to feed, too. I axed 'em was they goin' to carry the old cow over the winter, and they allowed they was. They ain't got nary a stable, and that poor critter lays out, and goes about bellerin', huntin' food. A heap of 'em does that way with their cattle. I'm sorry for the dumb things goin' round showin' their bones and huntin' food all winter, I can't hardly bear it. Cows can't give no milk unless they're took care of. It don't pay to keep 'em over winter, but folks goes on doin' it, and drawin' long faces in the spring about how poor they be. Same way with them as has steers and horses. They might get a good price for 'em in the fall, when the drovers comes through buyin' up cattle, but no, they won't sell 'em, though they, maybe, won't use 'em more'n two or three times all winter. Two year ago the Jakes done kept a horse and cow that way over winter. It were a mighty bad winter, too. The poor things was that weakly by spring that both on 'em died, and they ain't had money since to buy no more.

Sich folks draws dreful poor mouths, and goes about beggin' of them that's forehanded, and talkin' agin' 'em the worst way if they won't give nor lend 'em nothin'.

Old Mr. Cooke just goes for 'em when they git after him for corn. He allows as he were humpin' to work in the heat and cold to make a crap while some on 'em was settin' round the stores or bakin' their sides by the fire at home. He just won't lend 'em nary a thing. Some folks calls him hard names, but he's got his family to raise and he works mighty hard."

Mrs. Hansley remarked, as she noticed that the sky had clouded over: "The sun's mournin' for somethin'. I reckon we're goin' to have snow. I'd better be goin' along home. Good evenin'."

After she left, I replenished the wood fires, and resumed the writing she had interrupted. I forgot the weather 'til the fires burned low again and I felt cold. Then I saw, to my surprise, that the ground was white with snow. Before dark the wind rose to a gale, and the snowstorm became a blizzard.

We hugged the fire, thankful for warmth and shelter, and waked in our comfortable beds shivering when the wind shook the house and the trees whipped the roof.

II

"It's just a sight about them poor Dents," said Mrs. Hansley, a few days after the blizzard. "Lucky the neighbors had sent 'em warm clothes and victuals before the big snowstorm. They like to perished as it were. Mis' Dent says she reckons that old blanket you give her kept the baby from freezin'. She rolled him up in it, head and all, and kept him snugged up to her in bed all night.

You never see sich a place for folks to live in as where they're at. It's easy to say, 'Why don't they git out of it?' Them poor things is mighty hard pressed. Mr. Dent is one o' them kind as luck's always been agin'. Some says he drinks, but I ain't never see him the worse for liquor. A heap o' them that talks agin' him drinks a sight more nor he does. He's always kept his family on rented land, and most times he works it on shares. Can't neither him nor her, nor none o' them children, read and write, and folks gits ahead of him. Lots o' sich as he, when they work a place on shares, find their own share was mostly the hard work that went into the craps." Mrs. Hansley gave a harsh laugh, adding: "I been there myself. I'd oughter know.

Folks like the Dents get all out o' heart, and try another farm when they can't make nothin' for theirselves. That keeps 'em movin', and nobody can't blame 'em.

Work reg'lar, did you say? Him and the boys is mighty hard workin'. 'Pears like they'd oughter git along, but she's weakly, and they got sich a sight o' young 'uns. I reckon they can't never git enough victuals to fill 'em plum full, let alone clothes to keep 'em all covered at once.

I had more cornmeal than I were needin', so I stepped in, as I come by, to leave 'em some. They was right glad to get it, and I were right glad I toted it to 'em.

I never see sich a place. The wet o' the snow were all over the floor yet. You see, the door's off the hinges, and the windows is only boarded up loose. The roof ain't tight, and the chimney smokes.

When they see the storm comin' on bad, they got in all the wood they could tote, and made a good fire. They ain't got no stove, and it takes a right big fire to even touch sich a place as that. They sot the old table agin' the door, but he allows if the wind blowed it over onct it done it twenty times in the night, and every time the snow come bouncin' in like were bein' throwed, he says. 'Tain't no wonder the place 'pears like it'll never dry out.

Mr. Dent done told the rest of 'em to warm theirselves by the fire, and git into bed with their clothes on. They done it, and Mis' Dent even kept on her sunbonnet. He tucked 'em all in the best he could, and told 'em to lay close and go to sleep, and he'd set up and keep the fire goin'.

By that time the wind had rose and the snow come swirlin' in everywheres. I don't reckon there's a crack that's plum tight in that old shanty, anyhow. Before mornin' the beds and the floor was covered with snow. Mr. Dent had a brush broom, and he kept a-sweepin' a place in front of the fire with it all night. That were the best he could do, for he were nigh to perishin' every time he quit the

Chapter 13: Now is the Winter of Our Discontent

fire. I felt mighty bad when Mis' Dent were tellin' me about it. But, Lor' me! children's queer," Mrs. Hansley added, smiling. "While I were standin' at the door, a bird began chirpin' in a pretty green laurel-bush. One o' the boys was standin' there, and I says to him, by way of pleasant talk, that I wondered what the birds done the night of the big storm. He's a right peart young un. He give a quick look up into my face, and says, smilin', 'That's what I were thinkin' myself t'other night, when the snow were drivin' down on we-uns in bed.' It give me a kind of a turn to hear him," she said, with her eyes full of tears. "I kind o' ketched my breath, and says to myself, like I were prayin', 'Oh, Lord, I reckon this is one o' your little ones the Bible talks about.'

But what I came to tell you, 'cause I knowed you'd be glad to hear it, was that Mis' Dent done told me they're goin' to move off the mounting. Mr. Nye's got a right good house on one o' his farms, and he's goin' to put 'em into it, and they're goin' to work for him. He's mighty well-to-do, and if he takes a real interest in them poor Dents, it looks like they might get along now. My!, but them old pines is pretty with the snow shelvin' off 'em that way," said Mrs. Hansley, changing the subject. "Looks like, the way the wind blowed, the snow couldn't a' stuck to 'em, nohow.

That were a night to remember, and no mistake. I can't never forget the look o' the Dents' place. I'm mighty glad they're goin' to better theirselves," she said, as she went her way.

Sally

Once upon a time Henry Holt had been numbered with the Confederate dead. During the hours of merciful oblivion which followed the shattering of his right leg, his comrades, while hastily removing the wounded from the battlefield, had overlooked him.

When he awoke to conscious misery, there lay across his body, like a ghastly nightmare, the corpse of one of his mates. Filled with horror at the contact, he tried to throw it off. His arms still served him, but the effort to move his legs was torture. He could dimly hear distant firing, but the silence round about him was like a thick mist. Out of it came presently the commotion of struggle, followed by an unearthly groan. Turning his head, he saw close upon his left a wounded horse. One look convinced him that the poor creature was past help. With numbed hand he drew the pistol from the belt of the dead man; the next moment he was left the only living thing upon that bloody field.

"Poor old nag!" he sighed; "he'd have been some company in this hell of a place, but a body couldn't see a dumb critter suffer that way."

Then silence, except for the groans called forth by his own frantic efforts to get free from his burden. He fainted and came to many times before he succeeded. Then he fainted again when he tried to rise. When he came to himself he had sense enough to make a desperate effort to stanch the flow of blood from his wounded leg. This probably saved his life.

But we will let him tell his own story:

"I were that weak, for want o' food and drink and losin' so much blood, that I must have slep' away a heap of time before I took notice of a bugle-call and the tramp of men. Next I heard shovel and pick, and I know'd they was makin' ready to bury the dead. Weak and wanderin' in my mind like I were, that scared me. I put up my arms and tried to wave 'em, so's they'd see I were alive. I were too puny to holler. I couldn't see 'em, but it 'peared like I didn't care whether they was Yanks or our own boys.

The second time I got my arms up I heard voices, and then I see two Yankees lookin' down at me. 'Lord, Jim!' says the tallest one, 'this here Reb's alive. We must get him out of this sharp. Looks like he's done for.' Then I up and fainted again. Next I knowed I were in the Yanks' field hospital, and I hadn't but one leg. The doctors allowed I'd either got to die or lose my leg, so they cut it off. I didn't know nothing about it, and when I come to I just felt rested and comfortable.

Folks was right good to me, but I seed they was Yankees, and I allowed I were a prisoner. And so I were. When I got so's to be moved they sent me to Camp Chase, Ohio, and I was a prisoner there nigh about a year. It weren't no fun, but a body couldn't complain of nothin' but the eatin'. There were enough of it, sich as it were, but it weren't what we-uns had been used to. Some of us got to hankering to bile a pot. One of the Yankee subs – a mighty pleasant chap he were, too – heard us talkin' about it, and asked what it were. We done told him, and the next day the cook said as he had orders to let Bill Smedley and me come to the kitchen and bile a pot. Bill were wounded in the shoulder and were right puny.

We-uns was plum proud, I tell you. They give us a chunk of fat hog-meat, and while that were bilin', Bill and me got ready all the vegetables the cook give us, and then we put 'em all in with the meat. It weren't exactly like we-uns had at home, for there weren't no dried green beans, but it were nigh enough. It smelled so good that Bill and me and t'other fellers couldn't hardly wait to taste it.

It done us a heap of good to get somethin' like home again. After that, Bill and me used to help a sight in the kitchen, so's to get the cook to let us bile a pot now and then. It kind o' kep' us in heart. They done give us books and papers to read, and I let on to study

Chapter 14: Sally

over 'em. Them Yanks was mighty sharp-tongued about them as couldn't read and write, so I let on like I could.

One day I were settin' holdin' a book like I were readin', and a Yankee come along and give a great screehin' laugh that made me jump. 'Look here, you fellers!' he calls out, 'Johnny Reb's readin' with his book upside down!"

They all laughed fit to bust, and I were mighty mad inside, but I daresn't show it. I let on like I'd went to sleep while I were readin', and that's how the book come turned. After that I were careful to keep the big letterin' to the top. There's nothin' a body hates like havin' fun poked at 'em.

I hadn't my wooden leg then, and I hadn't got used to crutches, and I couldn't play no lively games like the rest. Time hung heavy first-off, and I sot round studyin' over my troubles a sight. Then I took to makin' baskets, like we-uns had at home. I swapped the first ones for tobacco, but I sold t'others. One way and another I picked up right smart money. I'd lost so much blood I were right white-lookin', and havin' but one leg, everybody were sorry for me; so I got more accommodation than some.

I allowed there wouldn't be nary a gal look at me, 'count of my wooden leg, when I came home. But, Lor' me! I needed two legs first-off to git away from 'em. Gals is plum curious creeturs. I were always kind of shy, and after a bit most of 'em quit follerin' me 'round, and I were glad of it.

My Sally always gits mad when I say she done the courtin', but it's nigh the truth. I were nothin' but a boy when I jined the army. I never did rightly know what the war were about. Most of 'em allowed it were for the niggers. I never sot no store by 'em, nohow, so that weren't what got me. It were the band, and the slick things the recruitin' officers told us. I reckoned it were mighty fine to go marchin' round to music, so I jined.

I were away two years, but I felt like I were ten years older when I come back. I were mighty downhearted first-off. You see, if a feller's been used to tearing round on two good legs all his life, it ain't easy to give in to crutches. No matter how kind t'other fellers mean to be, they can't help leavin' you out of everythin'. Why, when the fires used to get out I were always amongst the first to run, and I could work all day with the best.

Right after I got back, them lazy Kators, down in the holler, let their fires git out. The flames come licking up the side of the mounting like it were a flume. I seen 'em among the first, and started to run. Down I fell flat, and two fellers stopped and set me up again. I says to 'em: 'Go on, boys, for God's sake! Don't mind about me.' When they was clean out of sight, I laid flat on my face on the ground and cried like a baby.

That's where my Sally comes in. She come running along to the fire – she's that big and hefty now it makes a body laugh to think of her runnin', but she weren't that way then. There weren't another girl anywheres went trippin' about so light. I didn't hear her comin', 'count of the roarin' of the fire and the racket the boys was makin'. I weren't noways particular about cryin' soft, for I reckoned there weren't no one nigh enough to hear. I were too disheartened to care much, anyway.

First I knowed, an angel flopped down beside me – leastwise, that's what I though then – and had my head on her lap. Then she were a-cryin' too, and for about a minute we was both too fur gone to speak. It were Sally. 'Why, Henry,' she says, sobbing, 'I never knowed you felt that bad abut losing your leg. You always let on to be so kind of biggotty that we-uns allowed you was jest proud of it.'

'Oh, Lord, Sally! I ain't proud of nothin'. I'm miserable,' I groaned. Then I rolled my head up in her apron and cried out loud. Sally couldn't hardly get a corner to wipe her own eyes on.

After we was married, she owned up that she done hid that apron and let on to her folks like it were lost. She hadn't the heart to wash the tears out of it. For all I know she's got it yet. Sally's right romantic. After a bit we both felt better, and I sat up beside her, feeling kind of foolish. She looked at me and then she put her arms round my neck and kissed me.

'What do you mean by that, Sally?' I says, fer it kind o' scared me. Her face got red as fire, but she spoke up brave, 'It means that I love you, Henry,' she said.

You might have knocked me over with a rye straw. 'You don't mean you'd marry a poor cripple like me, Sally?' I says, catching my breath.

'Yes, I do, Henry,' she says, bursting into tears.

Then it were my turn to comfort her, and it's been turn and turn about between us ever since. Luck's been agin' us sometimes, but in the long run Sally and me's had things as comfortable as most.

When we was about to get married she allowed, seeing as I weren't no great on walkin' any more, we'd better live where we could see the mountings easy. 'Coves is good fer them as can climb,' says Sally, 'I've clomb out of 'em all my life, and thought nothin' of it, bein' so spry; but it's different with you, Henry. You'll want to see the mountings many's the time, to hearten you up.' I allowed as I wouldn't never need nothin' but her for that, but she only laughed. Sally's got a heap o' horse sense. 'Life's all ups and downs,' she says, 'and when you're down it's best to be livin' atop of the mountings, and not be in a cove, with 'em sort of on top of you.'

I hadn't never told nobody but her about the money I done saved up. It were enough to give us a start. We bought a rough piece of land, where there were a good spring, and her and me sot in to clear it. The neighbors poked fun at Sally for doin' it before we was married, but she allowed she knowed her own business.

When we got ready to build a little log house, the neighbors come forward mighty kind, and helped us. It weren't much of a house, but it were tight and snug, and there were a grand fireplace and chimney. We liked it splendid.

Sally knowed how to turn a place into a home along with the best, and she done it from the start. Folks used to come in wonderin' how it were that our place were a heap snugger than theirn. It were all Sally's contrivin'. She sot the house the way she wanted it, too. We hadn't no money to buy glass light for winders, but she had a big one cut out front and back, and put shutters on 'em for bad weather.

From the front winder and the door you could look way off over the mountings. You could see Hawk's Bill and Table Rock, like they was close by, and Grandfather Mounting, too; and clear days there were Roan and a sight of others standin' up against the sky. They was a heap of company, just like Sally said.

The Bible talks about mountings leapin' and singin', and I reckon there's somethin' in it. They always seem to be doin' somethin' different. When it's rainin' over there it's clearin' over here, and if you turn your back, it's like a spry gal that's changed her gown all in a minute. You can't never say just what the mountings *is* like, for before you git the words out, it's all different."

"But the winters must be dreary, aren't they?"

"Yes, we have pretty bad winters up here mostly, and I'm apt to get low in my mind along towards the last. I reckon that's why Sally's always watchin' out for the first turn of spring. First I know, when I'm settin' over the fire studyin', I hear her at the door callin' me to come out, she's got somethin' to show me. She's seen the spring beginnin' to work down in the valleys. She shows me them bright green spots here and there, and afterward I keep watch of 'em. First-off, they're clean down in the coves. Then the green comes creepin', creepin' up the mounting, while the snow's still layin' all round we-uns up here. On it comes, and before you know where you're at the snow's gone and the spring is busting all over the mounting, like folks laughin' out loud. 'Didn't I tell you so?' Sally says every time, and it does a body good to hear her laugh. 'There

126

can't no winter last forever,' she always says, but 'pears to me like it could. If it weren't for Sally heartenin' me up so, I reckon I'd shrivel up plum silly with the cold.

I ain't never been right stout since I lost my leg. You wouldn't believe it, but that very leg aches me so with the rheumatiz when the weather's cold that it's all I can do to bear it. If it weren't for Sally, I'd have give out long ago.

We had six children. Two of 'ems buried, but t'others was likely young 'uns. They're all married and gone now. Sally and me has the old house to ourselves mostly, except when our children's young 'uns come to stay with us. They're right fond of granny and me. Sally's always a-laughin', and that makes the young 'uns laugh, too.

It's been hard work scratchin' along sometimes, but she weren't never the one to give in, and we pulled through somehow. Folks calls us the 'old folks,' but Sally and me don't never feel old, and we don't allow to neither, not if we live to be a hundred."

Since Henry told his story he and his Sally have gone to that bourne whose prospective charms were nulled for him by Bible testimony that there was no marrying nor giving in marriage there.

He said he had "studied a heap" over that, and there couldn't be any heaven for him where he and Sally weren't going to be husband and wife.

Seeing how many wives some men had, he "allowed as things was mighty mixed, anyway," and it troubled him to the end.

Not so Sally. She was content to take it all on trust.

Chapter 15: Old Times

Old Times

Having heard that old Mrs. Yerkes was at variance with the Scripture doctrine about entertaining strangers, I made my first call upon her with diffidence. As she laid aside her pipe at my approach, and asked me to "take a cheer," I hoped she had modified her point of view, and regarded me in the light of a possible angel unawares.

The neighbors said everything depended upon her likes and dislikes. They were pretty sure to add that she was "right changeable and mighty apt to turn agin' a body next time," no matter how pleasant she had been at first. She evidently liked me this time, and much to my satisfaction, she was in a very talkative mood, so I made the most of the occasion.

Before she got started talking, however, she spent some time arranging her fire. It was made upon a plan quite new to me. The ends of two fence rails were thrust into the bed of glowing coals on the hearth, while their lengths lay stretched across the floor of the cabin. As they burned, she kicked or pushed them farther in.

"Old bones is cold bones," said she. "A body's bound to keep warm somehow. Sophrony's boys allows they tote a sight of wood for me, but it ain't enough to keep a chicken warm," the old woman added, scornfully. "Young folks is mighty unthoughted about doin' for the old folks. Sophrony's man hates it that bad my takin' the fence-rails that he's always jawin' about it. He don't say nothin' to me, though. He knows better. This here's my farm, and when I give in to their comin' onto it and puttin' up a house for theirselves I were sharp enough to have writin's drawed up," she laughed. "It's in them writin's as I'm to have all the wood I want to burn. I weren't goin' to have nobody tellin' me how much wood I needed. That's the way her folks done served old Mis' Grove. She allowed they reckoned as one stick a day were all she needed most times.

It don't hurt Sophrony's man none to take a spell at choppin' now and then. He's gettin' too fat." she added, laughing. "Hog-meat and buckwheat cakes, with a sight o' them molasses on 'em's right fattenin', let alone the way he sets round the stores and to home doin' nothin'. It would do a sight o'men good if they had to work the way folks done when my Ma and Pa come to the mountings. I don't reckon none on 'em was much fat them times. Everyways they turned they had to work mighty hard. I never see one o' them nice clearin's, where there ain't no stumps, and the crap or the grass grows so pretty, but I think o' the hard work them first settlers put into it first-off. I reckon there ain't no harder way o'puttin' in a day's work than grubbin'. 'Pears like some roots knows what you're doin' to 'em, and holds onto the ground to spite you.

My folks come up here from Virginny. It were gettin' too thick settled there for my Pa. So far as that goes, my Ma were about as bad as him. Neither one of 'em wanted to stay where folks was gettin' biggotty. Ma were alive when the boarder folks first came up here. Soon as she sot eyes on 'em, she allowed as they'd spile the whole country, and she were for movin' right off the mounting somewheres. Wouldn't none o' we-uns hear to it, though.

When her and Pa came up here it were all so wild that she had to learn to use a gun, just like the men folks. The woods was powerful thick, except in spots where fire'd got out. There weren't no real clearin's.

The folks that come to the mountings first hadn't never come so high up. They'd took up the bottom lands in the valleys, and worked 'em 'til they was drove off by the Indian. That were long before my folks come here."

"Then your folks have not been here many years, I suppose?"

"Yes, they was among the first that came clean up on the mountings. Bears was that plenty then they was meetin' up with 'em everywheres. Some on 'em wouldn't harm nobody, unless you pestered 'em, but folks had to watch out for their hogs. Hogs is

Chapter 15: Old Times

mostly right onhandy to catch, but bears is a heap smarter than they be. Ma allowed they liked fresh meat splendid, the way the hogs went sometimes.

She'd say we-uns didn't know nothin' about the bother o' gettin' along, 'count o' there bein' nothin' to pester the hogs and cattle when we turned 'em loose.

Ma'd tell how pretty it were to see the young bears playin together when they allowed nobody were nigh, but it were a sight the way the old she ones fit when they had cubs. They done killed some o' the first settlers." She paused to rearrange the fire. As I saw the rails growing visibly shorter, I speculated on the number of panels which would soon be missing from the nearest snake-fence if "Saphrony's man" didn't bestir himself to do that "chopping."

"The worst of rails," said the old woman, "is they're chestnut. There ain't no wood worse for snappin', and it beats everything for worms. The frost gets into the wormholes in winder, and when you go to burn it, it goes off like a gun sometimes. No, 'tain't right safe. I wisht I had some good mahogany or oak wood, but a body's got to do the best they can. Them big laurels is mighty fine to burn, but Sophrony takes all they bring in for her cook-stove."

While she was fixing the fire, I had been noting many things of interest in the windowless room. There was neither carpet nor mat on the floor, but the bed in the corner was covered with a homespun spread of red, white, and blue. It was quite a beauty, and the old woman told me with pride that she had woven it herself soon after her marriage. Some of the straight-backed, splint bottomed chairs had chintz covered cushions, which struck me as an unusual concession to comfort.

Strings of dried apples and small red peppers, interspersed with bunches of herbs and sage, came out fitfully in patches of harmonious color against the smoke darkened walls and beams, as the fire rose to a flame. When it died down again they fell back into obscurity, like the paling of stained glass in waning daylight.

"What were I tellin' you about – bears?" asked the old woman, after she had returned to her chair in the chimney-corner. "Well," she resumed, "first-off there weren't no doors to the houses. It were all the men folks could do to git up a log cabin with a stone chimbley. There weren't no sawmills, and they had to hew everythin' out with axes, except what little they could do with a hand saw. Them handmade shingles wore splendid, but they curled up powerful in a dry spell, and was mighty apt to leak bad.

The chimbleys smoked right bad, too, mostly. They hadn't nothin' but mud mortar to lay 'em up with, and it fell out a sight after they got het up. It worked out in wet weather, too. Cold nights they's hang a quilt, and most generally they sot saplin's across the doorway.

My hair always riz on my head, when I were little, when Ma'd git to tellin' how foxes and sich some in in the night. But I declare to goodness it were nigh to drappin' out when she'd tell how the bear come in.

Ma were layin' awake, and she heard him sniffin' round the door. Then he done pushed agin' the saplin's and down they went. That woke up Pa; didn't nobody sleep right sound them times, I reckon. He whispered for Ma to lay still. Then he reached for his gun, and when the bear got 'twixt him and the fire he done shot it. Pa were a might good shot. That bear never pestered 'em no more after the first fire. They had bear's meat a-plenty and to spare, and a big fur to keep 'em warm. Pa allowed it were time to get up some kind of a door after that, though. Ma hadn't no kind o' use for no newfangled ideas, and when she'd tell that story after she got old, she'd say she reckoned if it were now, she'd have been biggotty enough to put that big bearskin down on the floor for folks to walk on. She despised the very name of a carpet. She allowed as a good plank floor she could scour were good enough for her. An how Ma could scour a floor, when onct she got at it! She'd begin by twisting up her hair into a tight knot on top of her head, and pinnin' her gownd up to her knees. Ma had right pretty red hair when we-uns was little, and a sight of it, too, and a nice pink color in her cheeks.

After she'd got her gownd up out o' the way, she'd set all the chairs out o' doors, and by that time we-uns knowed what were comin'. Ma were right easy riled, and when she were busy we knowed better than to pester her.

If she felt right good, she'd let we-uns throw the sand all over the floor before she began to scour. We liked that part splendid. Most times she drove us off, though. Children's all alike, and bound to git to cuttin' up shines.

The best fun were seein' Ma put soft soap all round atop o' the sand 'til the floor were right slick with it. We-uns used to peek in the door, wishin' she'd let us slide round in it with our bare feet. I can feel the very way my toes kept wigglin' when I were wantin' to slide. When Ma weren't looking, we'd poke our feet into the soft soap nigh the door, but most like she'd git after us with a switch and run us off. After she'd begin to scour with that big hickory broom, and to sling water all about, we-uns knowed what to expect if we didn't clear out.

When I see her sweepin' the water out o' the door, I were always wishin' I were growed up, so's I could scour floors. I ain't found it sich a sight o' fun though," laughed Mrs. Yerkes.

After readjusting the burning rails in the fire, she said: "There was a heap o' wild critters besides bears goin' about when my folks come up here. There was wild cat and painters, and a body had a right to be afraid of 'em both. The men folks done shot a sight of 'em.

Deer was mighty plenty, too. They give Ma a big scare one night. All the neighbors had been grubbin' out roots all day. They was mostly them big ivy roots, mighty hard to git out, and hard to get shut of after you git 'em out. They make a right god fire, but they was too far from home for the men folks to tote 'em in; so they allowed they'd better pile 'em up in the clearin' and burn 'em 'long o' the brush. There ain't no puttin' of 'em out when onct they git afire, but the men folks throwed dirt over 'em when they quit work, 'count o' the wind risin' long toward night.

It were below our house, and before bedtime Ma'd got scarey about the fire gettin' out. Pa reckoned there weren't no sort o' danger, but nothin' wouldn't do Ma but that they'd take their guns and go down there and see for theirselves.

The fires was all right, just showin' like red and yaller lamps; but Ma see somethin' queer. She grabbed holt of Pa, and says, all shaky: 'Look at them big eyes nigh that farthest brush-heap Jedediah. It's the bad man his-self! O Lord, save us!" says she, drappin' on her knees and pullin' him down 'longside of her. 'There's more'n one of 'em; There's a sigh of 'em!' she says, beginnin' to cry. Sure enough, there was big eyes a-shinin' out o' the night all round them fires. By that time, Pa knowed what they be, and he up with his gun and fired. He done shot a big buck, but all the rest run off at the noise of the gun. Ma allowed she couldn't never forget the trip-trip o' the feet o' them deer goin' downhill in the night. 'Pears like sich wild critters is right curious about what folks is doin'," said Mrs. Yerkes. "They'll wait 'til the men quit work, and then steal into the clearin's to see; specially when there's fires like that night," she added.

"There was Indians round, too, when my folks come up here. They wasn't to say wild Indians. They was right peaceable. They mostly come up here to hunt and fish. There were right smart o' trout in the river them days. The sawmills has killed 'em out a sight, though. Them Indians lived way off. They'd bring up baskets and sich they made theirselves and trade 'em for victuals and things the folks up here had. Ma said the worst she had agin' 'em was their not wearin' more clothes when they went huntin' in warm weather. They never took notice who seen 'em, and Ma allowed they didn't know no better. She reckoned they felt as biggotty with just a string tied round their waists as she done when she got on a new wove gownd.

Chapter 15: Old Times

Folks done all their own spinnin' and weavin' in old times. Yes, and dyein's, too. Ma had the best indigo-blue dye-pot in the settlemint. The neighbors was always pesterin' her to lend it to 'em.

There weren't no print gownds, unless a peddler brung up the stuff, or some o' the men folks went clear way off to a big settlemint, and come back with a pack o' store goods on their backs. Ma said there weren't no roads them times, only wood-roads and trails, and the women folks was that uneasy about the men losin' their way while they was gone that they was willin' to do without store goods. Seein' how easy got most things is now, it's hard to believe how folks had to get along in old times.

To her dyin' day Ma always allowed they was a heap better off then then they be now. She reckoned as every new-fangled thing they got were somethin' more to take care of; just pilin' up worriment, she called it.

Pa nor her, neither one, didn't take no stock in eddicatin' children. They allowed as young 'uns was a sight better behaved when they hadn't no book learnin'. Did you say eddication ought to make 'em mannerly?" I don't reckon it's the book learnin' that spiles their manners; it's runnin' with bad children. There's a right smart o' that kind in school and everywheres. Them as can read and write gits a heap o' comfort out of it. I give ever one o' my children a right good chance o' schoolin'," Mrs. Yerkes said, getting up to attend to the fire.

"Was you askin' me what come o' Ma's old loom?" she said, as she sat down again. "It got bust up long ago, but that's her spinnin' wheel settin' there in the corner. Some boarder women come here tryin' to buy it. I axed 'em what they allowed to do with it. They done said they wanted it to put in their parlor to look at. I reckoned I'd keep it to look at myself. I weren't so struck on it when I were young, though, and Ma'd set me to work at it. Children was raised to work them days. I can hear Ma now sayin', 'If you-uns don't quit your foolin', and git to work, I'll know the reason mighty quick!"

When there weren't nothin' else to do, she kept us knittin' stockin's and mittens.

The boarders is mighty pesterin'. I dunno how many of 'em's been after me to sell 'em that there bedspread, and maybe you wouldn't believe it, but some on 'em come in yesterday wantin' to buy that cupboard in the corner!" she exclaimed, in disgust. "I don't reckon they'll come again. I got right mad at 'em. My old man made that cupboard out of a big wild cherry-tree he done cut down and sawed up his own self when we was first married. He does all the work on it evenin's, too, so I seen him puttin' every stick of it together. Time enough when I'm dead and gone for folks to be comin' after my things," said Mrs. Yerkes, giving the rails an extra hard push that sent the flames dancing up the chimney. A sudden transformation was wrought in the simple room, as new form and color took shape in the flashing light.

"My old man made that set o' drawers you're lookin' at, too, and like as not some o' the boarders'll be wantin' to buy them next," she snapped.

"'Pears like some on 'em allows as money'll buy anythin'. They'll find out different if they come pesterin' me much more.

Did you say would I show you some o' Ma's weavin's? S'pose I'll have to, but it's mighty unhandy gettin' at 'em," she said, ungraciously, as she gave the rails another shove into the heart of the fire. Then getting slowly down upon her knees, she began pulling an old trunk from under the bed. As she scorned my offer of assistance, I feared she was mentally classing me with the "pesterin' boarders."

The trunk, upon being opened, presented a very helter-skelter interior. Mrs. Yerkes, however, seemed to have a good mental inventory of its contents, most of which she tossed out upon the floor, making audible comments as she did so. Finally she pulled out the "ging-gums" she was in search of.

Chapter 15: Old Times

One piece was a bedspread in huge blue and white check. It looked as if it might last forever, so I inquired why it was not in use.

"Don't want it to wear out," she replied. "Ma sot a heap o' store by the things she'd wove. She done used that spread on her bed nigh about twenty year, and I'm bound to make it last my time. These here's her dress and aprons."

All of the "weavin's" she had shown me were blue-and-white ginghams.

"Her and me done wore out the woolen things," said Mrs. Yerkes, "except the stuff in this old brown skirt I got on. Ma done wove that."

She allowed me scant time to examine the ginghams before she began hustling the things back into the trunk, which she shut with a bang, and hastily pushed into its place under the bed.

"You see, I'm afraid some o' Sophrony's young 'uns might come in," said she. "They're always pesterin' me to give 'em them things. They sha'n't have nary one of 'em while I'm above ground. Ma'd turn in her grave, I do believe, if them gals of Sophrony's was to go trapseing around in her things. Not but what they're nice enough gals," she added, hastily, as she remembered that they were her grandchildren. "Folks is mighty good and kind, but times is changed."

She sighed. "I used to laugh at Pa and Ma for talkin' so about the good old times, but I reckon they wasn't fur wrong," said she.

The rails were now consumed to a length which permitted her to use them as ordinary sticks on the fire. She threw some brush on top of them, and as it leaped into a blaze she took up her pipe and began to refill it.

I understood this was a signal that she was tired of entertaining strangers. I rose at once to go, and was rewarded for my promptness by a cordial invitation to come again.

Getting an Education

I

The room was so low that a tall man could not stand upright in it without bumping his head against the hewn rafters, but the fire of green logs, well alight, sent abroad a ruddy glow and dancing shadows that transformed the commonplace and softened all harsh outlines.

As there were no windows in the cabin, the light was not strong enough to throw into relief the bald bareness of the room, nor the scanty wardrobes of the family sitting near the fire.

"Be you goin' to mill to-morrow, Pa?" asked the eldest girl. " 'Cause if you be, I want to go 'long. I got some store errands to do for Ma."

"Yes, Nancy, I be," replied her father; "but I don't like your goin' so often to the settlemint. Folks is powerful hands to talk. First you know, they'll be sayin' you're courtin' some feller over there. I don't want no gal o'mine talked about, mind you."

"Shucks!" exclaimed Nancy, scornfully. "Let 'em talk; who cares?"

"Let her be, Por," said the mother, reaching for her snuff-box. "Gals is gals, and they're bound to enjoy theirselves a bit. Nance is all right."

That settled it, and the next morning Nancy, seated on the bags of corn, rode off in the ox-cart with her father. While he was gone to the mill, she did her store errands, but when he returned she did not speak of the one she considered of the most importance.

At supper time her father asked, suddenly: "Who were that stuck-up chap I see you talkin' to, Nancy, when I come back from the mill? I plum forgot him 'til this minute."

Nancy wished he'd forgotten him altogether. She was tired, and felt unequal to what she knew was coming. Her face flushed as she replied, testily: "He ain't stuck up, neither. You always allow as every one's stuck up as wears store clothes. That's Sam Burke, come back from college. He knows a sight. He's goin' to teach the Wren Hill school this winter, and I'm goin' to it, too. He says I ain't too old to learn if I be fifteen."

Her father, busy shoveling fried potatoes into his mouth, laid in an extra supply before grounding his arms, with his knife and fork grasped in clenched fists, while he looked at Nancy.

Without waiting for him to speak, she burst forth: "You can't scare me like you onct could, Pa, lookin' at me that way. 'Cause I'm nigh about as big as you be now," added she, laughing nervously. "When I were little I wanted to go to school, 'long with t'other gals, but you always had excuses for keepin' me at home. There were always a sight of work for me to do, and I done it, but I never got no schoolin'! *Now* I'm goin' to get a eddication."

"Oh! You be, be you?" snarled her father. "Well, just tell me who's goin' to keep you while you're gittin' it."

"I ain't never said I weren't goin' to work no more," began Nancy.

"Work!" retorted her father; 'gals as goes to school ain't worth the shoe-leather they wears out trompin' the roads."

"Shoe-leather, indeed!" rejoined the girl, sharply. "There ain't nary another gal as big as me goin' mostly barefoot, and I ain't never had no rightly good gownd in my life. And no more ain't Mor," added Nancy, quickly, as she caught her mother's sympathetic glance.

"You ain't no call to talk that way to me, nohow, Por," she went on, hurriedly. "You and Mor knows I've carried wood and water

140

Chapter 16: Getting an Education

ever since I could tote 'em, and you ain't never done a batch o' clearin' but what I helped with. I've heard you brag many's the time how peart I be to handle a ax when I weren't no bigger nor Janie here." Janie was four years old.

As Nancy was still given the floor, she went on: "I allow I've earned my bread by the sweat of my brow, and Lord knows I ain't had much else! I reckon women's made for somethin' besides always slaving for men folks. The boarders is always pokin' fun at we-uns, and sayin' why don't we strike, whatever that be. I allow it's somethin' to do with a eddication. Anyway, I'm bound to git one."

Her father still regarded her in silence, and she continued: "No, you ain't no call to talk about shoe-leather to me, Por, but when it comes to that I tell you right now I've done got it all fixed. I went to see Mr. Comber to-day, and he 'lows he can make me all the shoes I want. His wife's weakly, and I'm going to pay for 'em by washing for her."

This was the important errand which was to settle the school question for Nancy. Her meeting with the new teacher had been purely accidental, and their brief conversation a business affair. Not that the interview had not added a touch of romance to her new undertaking, for in his improved appearance and speech and "store clothes" he seemed to Nancy's simple mind a very superior being. As her father still said nothing, she went on: "I'm plum tired of bein' laughed at by the boarders. A boarder lady asked me t'other day what work I did, and I said I done holped you and Mor, and she laughed, and said there weren't no sich word as *holped*."

"Yes, there be, too," spoke up Mrs. Rivers, "for I done heerd preacher readin' it outen the Bible, Sunday were a week. I 'low she's one of them infidels as ain't got no religion and don't never read the Bible."

"No, she ain't, neither," retorted Nancy; "she's a right good lady." Nancy felt bound to defend this particular boarder lady, whose friendly interest had done much to stimulate the girl to strike for an education.

All this time Mr. Rivers, still holding his knife and fork in rigid fists, sat staring at Nancy, the greasy potatoes grown stone cold upon his plate. His wife's danger signals, given by means of a kick or two under the table, served to hold in check his impulse to knock the girl down on the spot. He was a hard man in his own family, but heretofore there had been no open rebellion.

His wife, an easy-going creature, with a figure like a meal-sack, was not calculated by temperament to inspire her husband or children to do their best, but she was peaceable, and hated a fuss of any kind, and was in misery now lest Nancy and her father come to an open rupture. As soon as she could attract Nancy's attention, she said, pointedly: "Nance, I wish you and the children would go and git in the light wood for mornin'; I plum forgot it."

Nancy, glad of a respite, rose hastily to do her bidding, and the other children trooped out at her heels. Sending them off into the new clearing to gather pine-chips, Nancy, resting her arms on the top rail of the fence, turned her face toward the mountains, which were always her solace in time of trouble. The sun had set, and every purple peak and rugged outline stood clear-cut against the canary-colored sky. Far up in the zenith floated clouds still glowing crimson and gold, while the world beneath lay in shadow. From her infancy Nancy had been a regular attendant at church and Sunday-school, and was familiar with the noble poetry and beautiful similes of the Bible, and her own mind was full of dumb imagery. Glancing upward, she saw the shining clouds, and her face brightened. "It's like them that see a great light," she said, softly, to herself, "and we-uns is like them that sits in darkness. I'm bound to git into the light, if I can, but I reckon sassin' Por ain't the way to begin."

After the children had left the room, Mrs. Rivers said to her husband: "Nance is mighty like you, Reuben; she's got a heap of horse sense, but when she gits the bit in her teeth and takes to pullin',

Chapter 16: Getting an Education

mout as well give her her head." Mr. Rivers swallowed the bait, and laughing grimly, resumed his attack upon the fried potatoes.

"'Tain't no feller as has done it," resumed his wife; "it's the boarders. She sees their gals so nice and fixy, and pretty-spoke, and she thinks it's all along of their having eddication. She'll find out her mistake; poor folks has always got to work, but it ain't no use tryin' to check her up now. The mischief's done."

Although Mr. Rivers had a fine masculine scorn of the other sex, he knew by experience that his wife was generally in the right; so he gulped down the hot coffee she poured for him, and finished his supper in silence. When Nancy and the children returned, he was peaceably smoking his pipe in the chimney-corner. Nancy and her mother washed the few supper dishes in silence, and then the whole family retired for the night. Nancy, hoping that her point was gained, was too excited to sleep. She lay awake, listening to the heavy breathing of the rest as one after another fell asleep.

The fire, which had been covered with ashes, suddenly fanned by a puff of wind, sent a shower of cinders upon the bare floor. This was of too common occurrence to disturb Nancy, but presently she smelled something burning, which made her rise on her elbow and look around the room. Then she sprang up in alarm. A spark lodging close to her parent's bed, which stood near the fireplace, had caught the corner of a cotton comfortable hanging down to the floor, and a tongue of flame was rapidly creeping upward. Nancy made no outcry, but seizing the water-bucket, quickly put out the fire without disturbing the sleepers.

Before discovering it she had been too busy building air-castles to notice the rising of the wind, which now shook the cabin and drove the smoke in fitful gusts down the chimney.

"Sich an awful night for a fire!" she said to herself; "and supposin' Por had got burnt up, I'd have felt powerful bad about sassin' him that way. All the same, I got as good a right to git an eddication as other gals; but I'm mighty glad I were laying awake when the fire cotched."

In the morning, when it became evident that she had saved the house, and perhaps the family also, from an untimely end, Nancy found herself treated with unusual consideration. Whatever her father thought of her undutiful behavior at supper-time, he made no reference to it.

II

Nancy had thought her troubles at an end when her father tacitly withdrew his opposition, but her first day at school convinced her to the contrary.

Sam Burke, the new teacher, was making his own struggle for an education. It was not made easier for him by having to do his first teaching so near home. The school he had attended, though dignified by the name of college, was a very poor affair. After two winters spent in mastering its curriculum, he had come forth so shaky as to what he must now try to impart to others that he entered upon his new duties in fear and trembling. This necessitated his putting on a show of dignity and severity, which for a time made him very unpopular in the school.

He made a great point of examining the pupils in order to grade the classes. As he began with the older ones, poor Nancy's turn came all too soon. She quaked in her stiff new shoes as she listened to the questions put to those who preceded her, and heard the bursts of ridicule which greeted many of the answers. At this time Sam himself was not above sitting in the seat of the scorner. When her name was called, Nancy stumbled up to his desk in a state of alarm, and was quickly relegated to the infant class.

Chapter 16: Getting an Education

She tramped back to her place amid laughs of derision, muttering to herself, as she glanced around the room, "'Tain't my fault I don't know anything. I ain't never had nary a chance. Just wait and see if I don't beat 'em all yet!"

Then she burst into tears. This new diversion for the idlers brought them crowding around her, and the teacher, who said angrily that he couldn't hear himself think, ordered all who had already been examined to leave the room. This, of course, included Nancy. The moment she was outside of the schoolhouse her courage returned, and she proceeded to pitch into those who had ridiculed her, establishing once for all her right to get an education with the best of them.

But her real difficulties began the next day, when sitting in class with the younger pupils she for the first time in her life attempted a simple lesson in Webster's "Speller." The smallest child in the class had far less difficulty than had Nancy in remembering the letters. They blurred so before her eyes that the simplest of three-lettered words became hopeless puzzles to her unaccustomed senses. So bewildered did she become at last that she didn't even know the meaning of words like "cat" and "dog" when given out by the teacher.

The other pupils, mindful of the lesson she had given them the previous day, did not dare to laugh, but they were so diverted watching her that the teacher, who was finding his own position no sinecure, got very impatient at their inattention, and calling them "a stupid lot," ordered them to their seats.

Nancy's bitterness of heart would have been much mitigated could she have known that he was only giving them a rehash of his own school experiences. As it was, she was so angry and so humiliated that had she not feared the ridicule of her father and the neighbors she would then and there have given up her attempt to get an education, and gone back to her work, content to be a hewer of wood and a drawer of water for the rest of her days.

While fiercely regarding the recalcitrant letters in her spelling-book, however, she had a brilliant idea, which she put into execution on her way home. She took her book to the 'boarder lady' whose washing she was now doing, and boldly stated her difficulties.

"I 'lowed you knowed most everything, Miss Thompson," said Nancy, "and you're so kind I knowed you wouldn't mind telling me what was the matter with these pesky letters. I'm beat if I can tell which side's up or down."

Miss Thompson, who liked the girl, was glad to give her a lift, and thanks to her help, Nancy was soon at the head of the infant class. Early and late she was poring over her book, and for a time at least she was, as her father put it, not worth her salt at home.

The teacher's attention had from the first been centered upon a pretty girl two years older than Nancy. Her people were sufficiently well-to-do to give her whatever educational advantages came in their way, and to dress her better than her companions.

She scorned Nancy and her humble abode, so they had little in common. Nancy said of her; "If Amorita Topknot will just go her own way, I sha'n't pester her; she's too biggotty for me."

Amorita's way appeared for a while to be a very flowery one, for the new teacher made everything easy for her. In fact, he fell heels over head in love with her, and for a time so neglected his duties to the other pupils that the Board privately voted to turn him out if he did not mend his ways.

About this time a young man as old as Sam Burke himself came to school, and presently he began to cast admiring glances at Nancy.

This did not suit Amorita, who was of a jealous disposition, and resented attentions paid to other girls. So, regardless of the fact that she was now privately engaged to Sam, she made a dead set at Evans Dower, the new pupil. Heretofore, in order to be alone with the teacher, she had waited, when school was dismissed, 'til the rest were gone, but now she was first to leave, and it was not her fault if she did not walk part of the way home with Evans.

Nancy's mind had been so taken up with the difficulties which beset her every step on the highway of education that she had given little heed to what was going on around her, and she was entirely oblivious of Evans Dower's admiration for herself. She had, to be sure, often wished that the teacher would give her as ready assistance as he bestowed upon Amorita; but she thought it only natural that so backward and stupid a pupil as herself should receive very little attention from any one.

But presently Nancy awoke to the fact that some sort of a change had come over the teacher. For a while he had been very irritable over the blunders of the pupils; then he became listless and indifferent, and poor Nancy was often at a loss to know whether she had recited correctly or made another failure. Her attention once aroused, she began to observe Sam, and she decided he must be sick.

"Don't you allow it's the fever workin' on him, Mor?" she asked her mother. "He's plum sallow, and peaked-lookin', and he don't take no interest in anything. He used to be always helping Amorita with her lessons. Now he don't scarcely notice her, and she's that sassy to him sometimes I'd like to slap her, but he don't say nary a word back. And the young 'uns is getting to cut up such capers that a body can't hardly study in school, but he don't seem to mind."

Mrs. Rivers laughed. "More like he's in love, Nancy," she said. "Who's he been courtin'? That Amorita?"

"La, Mor, I ain't never though of that. I've been so took up with my books I warn't taking notice of what was going on round me. But, that's better than fever, ain't it, Mor?"

"Dunno," replied her mother, shaking with laughter; "folks gits over the fever, if they don't eat too much truck and die with it, but love-sickness goes hard sometimes."

This aroused Nancy's interest and sympathy, and the next day she picked out the finest apple she could find, and polished it carefully, and slyly laid it on Sam's desk. It had the desired effect. The poor fellow, thinking it a peace offering from Amorita, made a great parade of eating it with relish at recess, although all the morning she had turned him the cold shoulder. Nancy, finding the atmosphere a little cleared, decided to place a friendly offering of some sort upon Sam's desk every few days. He, accepting them all as he had done the first, began to appear like himself once more, although Amorita no longer smiled upon him.

During this interregnum the snapping of apple-seeds and the firing of slimy spitballs had been the order of the day, the pre-occupied teacher being the target for many of the missiles. It was a trying time for Nancy. She was too studious to escape notice of the idlers, who hit her many a stinging filip. She had her trials at home, too, for even her easy-going mother was getting tired of her long absences and of trying to make the other children do her work. One day, after she had been going to school about a month, her father brought home the county paper, and ordered her to read to him.

"Why Pa!" exclaimed Nancy, aghast, "I ain't got so fur as to read real readin' like that, and you'd ought to know it."

"What be you goin' to school for, then, if you ain't learnin' to read, write, and cipher?" snapped her father.

"So I be," replied Nancy, eagerly, "but I ain't learn't yet. You've got to give a feller time."

Scenes like this were of frequent occurrence. Nancy was often put to it to keep the peace at home, while things dragged so wearily in school that she got quite disheartened.

Amorita's devices to win the regard of Evans Dower were not a success. He told some of the boys that Nancy was worth six of her. This, being duly reported to Amorita, made her pursuit of him the more eager, for it was always the unattainable which had the higher

Chapter 16: Getting an Education

value in her eyes. So she continued to torment the teacher by her attention to Dower, while Sam, like herself, became the more keen after what seemed slipping from his grasp. One day he ventured to hint to the girl that if she were so indifferent to him as she now claimed to be, she wouldn't be placing love-tokens upon his desk, at which she flew into a towering rage, flatly denying the charge. She was so evidently in earnest that he was forced to believe her. This, for a time, seemed to knock the foundations from under him.

As Nancy's offerings were now left unheeded upon his desk, she brought no more for some time. Seeing that he was greatly troubled about something, however, she longed to help him. She was herself so sensitive to the charm of flowers that she wished it were summer, that she might bring him some. As the next best thing, she tried a bunch of wintergreen, with its bright red berries glowing amid the glossy dark leaves. She saw the teacher take it up listlessly, and pick off a few of the berries, eating them in absent fashion.

Next she essayed a wreath of the beautiful red and bronze galax-leaves, similar to one she had seen Miss Thompson making. She slipped it into school under her apron, and laid it upon Sam's desk. So far she had escaped detection, but her offering had attracted the notice of the other pupils, and at sight of the wreath there was a general buzz of interest.

The teacher, who seemed to have himself well in hand this morning, after holding it up for general admiration, hung the wreath upon a nail over his desk. He said he was very much obliged to the unknown donor, and that it served as a reminder of something he had intended to speak of before. This was that during the Christmas holidays he proposed to invite the parents of the pupils to the schoolhouse to listen to recitations and examinations, and he should like to have the room decorated with wreaths and evergreen for the occasion. And he added that from this time on they should devote an hour each afternoon in preparing for this event.

He was very cheerful, and told his plans in a bright, earnest way that aroused the interest and stimulated the ambition of the pupils. Nancy was puzzled to account for this sudden change in him, but Amorita, who looked very downcast, could have explained it. The truth was, Sam, having reached the limit of endurance, had demanded of Amorita the previous evening a full explanation of her changed attitude toward himself. She had resented his air of authority, and given tantalizing replies to his questions, which in turn aroused his ire. In a few moments they had passed the rapids and were in the whirlpool of a violent lover's quarrel.

Amorita declared their engagement at an end, and Sam discovered, to his surprise, that this was what he most desired.

Now that the suspense and irritation of the past few weeks were over, he applied himself with commendable zeal to his work in the schoolroom, while Amorita was left to chew the cud of bitterness, having lost the old lover and failed to captivate the new. All that Nancy perceived was that Sam paid much more attention to the classes. This enabled her to get on so much faster with her lessons that she was even losing her dread of the approaching examinations.

Miss Thompson, who had volunteered to teach her a piece for recitation, had taken great pains with her. Nancy tried her best to follow all of her direction, as well as the hints she gave her about dress and arrangement of her abundant hair.

When the great day arrived her parents were surprised to find themselves so proud of her.

Amorita upon this occasion, while eclipsing all the rest in dress, failed to distinguish herself otherwise, and went home in the sulks. Most of the students acquitted themselves with credit, however.

Nancy, seeing that the teacher was for some reason no longer an object of sympathy, made the wreath her final offering. In puzzling for a time over the identity of the donor, he did not think of Nancy. Although civilly kind to the girl, he, in common with many others,

Chapter 16: Getting an Education

regarded her family as of "no account," and though himself above her. She had, to be sure, won his respect by her plodding perseverance; nor had he failed to note the steady improvement in her personal appearance, as her brain, so long dormant, began to assert itself.

Glimpses caught of her face, full of vivid interest in her work, often reminded him of the old book of fairy stories he was fortunate enough to own in his childhood. He wondered if it were not the kiss of Knowledge which, after all, awakened the Sleeping Beauty. Miss Thompson's influence had told upon Nancy in many ways. She had in consequence become much more tidy in dress and person. Her fine head of hair now gave ample evidence of familiarity with brush and comb, and her well-kept teeth added charm to a ready smile. Taken altogether, with its good skin, fresh color, and sincere eyes, Nancy's face was a very attractive one.

Sam, much to his annoyance, discovered that his eyes kept straying in the direction of a sunny head bent studiously over a book. He was vexed if Nancy chanced to glance up at such times, although she did it in absent fashion, as she memorized her lessons. That vexed him, too. He had been so used to Amorita's devices to attract his attention in the early days that he resented Nancy's indifference. "I might be a stock or a stone, the way she looks at me with those eyes of hers," he often said to himself.

This made him the more eager to capture her personal liking, and he went out of his way to help her with her lessons. Nancy accepted these attentions gratefully, but was wholly obtuse as to the feeling which prompted them.

Knowing but too well in what contempt her family were held by many of their neighbors, she supposed that Sam Burke shared the same prejudice, and she had never thought of him in the light of a possible lover. In truth, he himself would have scoffed at such an idea at this time. But in spite of himself, he was becoming desperately interested in the girl, and in deadly fear lest she or others find it out.

With the money he should receive for his winter's work he meant to continue his own education at the Highbridge Academy. Like a reckless moth, he thought he might flit around the candle 'til that time, and then soar away with wings unsinged. And so he might for all Nancy cared, for she was making such rapid progress with her lessons that her whole attention was concentrated upon them.

Amorita, finding useless her efforts to recaptivate Sam, soon discovered that his heart had been caught in the rebound.

"And by stupid Nancy Rivers, of all girls!" she said to herself. "Never mind! I'll soon settle him."

She began by making slighting remarks about Nancy in Sam's hearing, but as this had no effect, she changed her tactics. She now made advances to Nancy, who, however, fought shy of her for a long time, but was at last won over by her persistent professions of friendship. After this, they walked to and from school together, which gave Amorita the chance to enlarge upon her love affair with Sam. She represented him as having deceived her cruelly, and Nancy was moved to many expression of eager sympathy or sharp indignation. Amorita saw to it that some of these came to Sam's ears.

He had watched this increasing intimacy between the two girls with growing uneasiness, but was powerless to check it. It's effects were soon visible in Nancy's attitude toward himself. Amorita had assured her that his only object in giving her so much extra assistance with her lessons was that he might win her affections and then cast them aside, as he had done her own. In place of its former friendly unconsciousness, Nancy's manner toward him now assumed the mildly defensive.

Amorita, overjoyed at Sam's evident chagrin, redoubled her devotion to Nancy, whom, now that she seemed beyond his reach, he thought grown prettier and more attractive each day. Her speech , too, was daily improving, and he hardly noticed the slips of her tongue, so glad was he to listen to her soft voice.

He was constantly contrasting her with Amorita, who now seemed to him so flashy and course that he marveled he could ever have been in love with her. Nancy had become to him the pearl of great price, for the possession of which he often felt ready to barter his very soul. How was he to live without the daily sight of her after school closed, had become his most absorbing problem.

III

At the noon recess one bitter cold day, when the whole school, the teacher included, were gathered about the overheated stove, the boys began skylarking, and in the rough play Nancy was thrown against the stove.

For an instant she was conscious of the blistering heat and a sharp pain in her arm, but the next minute she was being swiftly borne to a seat. Then some one was leaning over her, and in great agitation asking if she were much hurt. Nancy looked up in amazement into the face of the teacher, and something she read there caused her eyes to overflow as the pain of the burn increased.

"Is it so bad?" he whispered; and the next moment there was a thud, and Sam lay at her feet in a dead faint.

The school was in an uproar in an instant. The children's nerves, unstrung by Nancy's accident, were now jangling in all keys. Amorita, too, added to the confusion by throwing herself on her knees beside Sam, wringing her hands and weeping audibly. Evans Dower had been almost as much demoralized as the teacher himself. Nancy was the first person in the room to recover self-control.

She sent the younger children to their seats, and asking Dower to bring water, she bathed Sam's face, telling Evans to loosen his collar, and the rest of the pupils to stand back and give him air. Then she suggested that as he might take cold if left upon the floor 'til he came to, some of the bigger boys should lay him upon the long bench at the back of the room.

One of her brothers had fainting fits, so she was not a novice in the treatment of them. As no one took any notice of Amorita, she returned to her seat near the fire. Upon second thought she had concluded not to give Sam himself the benefit of a scene. When he at last opened his eyes they rested upon the anxious face of Nancy.

"You're better now, ain't you?" she asked, hurriedly.

"Yes, I'm all right," he replied, trying to rise; "but you, were you terribly burned? Oh, my God! it was awful!" he cried, unmindful of any presence but hers.

"Pshaw!" said Nancy, lightly, "it wasn't so bad as all that. It's my gown I'm thinking about; see here, my sleeve's burnt clean through," she added, smiling, "and so's the front breadth of my skirt."

As he glanced at her sleeve, Sam turned so pale that Nancy, thinking him about to faint again, wished she had known better how to divert his attention from her burned arm, which was paining her so badly that she could scarce restrain her tears. Sam, fallen back upon his pillow of coats, was regarding her with such earnestness that she grew uncomfortable, and made a motion to withdraw.

"Don't go, Nancy!" he whispered, clutching at her gown.

Then suddenly remembering where they were, he said, in a tone of authority: "All of you go to your seats and your lessons. I'm thankful for your kindness; I'll be all right in a minute, when my head stops spinning."

Nancy started to obey with the rest, but found herself held fast.

Chapter 16: Getting an Education

"Don't go, Nancy," pleaded Sam, softly. "I thought it was all over with you, and I'd never have a chance to tell you I loved you. That's why I fainted afterward."

Nancy, wholly unprepared for such an avowal, and fast weakening with pain, dropped into a seat beside him.

"What a brute I am!" he whispered, trying in vain to rise. "Say you forgive me, Nancy, for forgetting your bad burn and keeping you here when you ought to be on your way to the doctor's to get it dressed."

"Yes, yes," replied Nancy, softly; "I ain't blaming you, teacher," (Sam winced at the word) "but it's all come on me so sudden that I've got to get away by myself to think. I'll go to the doctor's now. My arm does hurt awful," she added, rising, while the tears began to stream down her cheeks.

"You sha'n't go alone, Nancy," replied Sam. "Wait just a minute 'til I can stand, and I'll go along. I need medicine myself," added the artful youth. She waited, but with averted face.

They took the short cut through the woods, and Sam drew her hand through his arm, gently wiping her fast-welling tears with his handkerchief; but not 'til they neared their destination did he speak.

"I don't ask you to say anything to-day, Nancy," he said at last. "It came on me most suddenly as it has on you. I knew I cared for you, but I thought you didn't like me, and I didn't mean to speak. Just say you forgive me for startling you so when you were so badly burned."

"Yes, yes, I do, Sam" (Sam smiled, as his name slipped out); but please don't say anything more," replied Nancy, in an agitated voice.

They were silent the rest of the way. When the doctor set Sam to cutting the sleeve from Nancy's injured arm, it was she who broke the silence between them.

"It's all right, Sam," she said, as she saw him turn deadly pale when the great burn was revealed. "It ain't so powerful bad. Doctor's got such kind hands he won't hurt a mite more than he can help, and I can bear it."

The doctor glanced at Sam over his spectacles. "It seems to me you're easy upset, young man; you wouldn't do for a doctor. Here, I'll give you something that will set you up," he said.

"That's good of you," returned Sam. "I haven't felt right well lately. I came along with Nancy to consult you."

Glancing kindly from one to the other, the doctor replied, with a smile, "I don't think you need any more of my medicine, Sam." Nancy's face flushed, and Sam laughed nervously, but the doctor was at that moment giving his whole attention to the dressing of Nancy's burn.

She was quite feverish and ill for three or four days, unable to sit up, and her parents were much flattered that the teacher should stop night and morning to inquire about her, but Nancy made no comment. On the afternoon of the fifth day there was a gentle "Come in," in response to his knock, and on pushing open the door, he saw that Nancy was alone, sitting near the fire. He hurried to her side, and with gallantry born of love, raised her hand to his lips and kissed it reverently.

"Oh, no, don't! don't, Sam!" cried Nancy, in distress.

"And why not?" he demanded, still holding the hand.

"Because I've done thought it all over since I've been sick, and you must quit thinking about me. Your people would never give in to your marrying me," Nancy replied.

"And suppose they wouldn't?" queried Sam, releasing her hand long enough to get a chair on which to seat himself beside her, when he promptly resumed its custody, and kissed it again.

Chapter 16: Getting an Education

"But you mustn't do that, Sam, and you mustn't sit so close, either; somebody might come in."

"Let 'em come," returned Sam, cheerfully. "I've only been waiting to get a chance to see you alone before making a clean breast of it to your father and mother, and then I don't care who knows."

"But I'm too young," began Nancy. "And you needn't think I don't know how folks look down on we-uns for living like we do," she added, rapidly, her improved English taking to itself wings.

"I don't see what that's got to do with you and me," answered Sam, sturdily.

He had had his struggle in the days of his dawning love for Nancy, and as is often the case, love had speedily silenced reason and prudence.

"It's got a heap to do with us," returned Nancy. "I don't allow as anything will ever change Pa and Ma; but I'm bound to get an education first-off, and after that I've got to help the children to get one, too. So you see I couldn't marry you if I wanted to."

"I know you're young, Nancy, but I'm afraid you will have time enough to grow older, and to educate yourself and the children, too, before I can afford to marry; but just say you *want* to marry me, and we'll settle all the rest afterward," replied Sam, regarding her earnestly. Nancy's frank eyes returned his gaze for an instant, and then fell before his more ardent ones. She flushed deeply, and paled again, but did not speak.

"Say it, Nancy, dear," pleaded Sam, pressing her hand between his own.

"I can't," faltered she; "I heard right queer things about you before you – before the day I got burned, so what you said came too sudden, and I'm all scared-like ever since."

"Yes," replied Sam, "I can guess what you heard. I don't want to talk against Amorita, but it was her doings, I know." Nancy made no reply.

"I'll tell you the whole story," Sam went on. "I haven't got any sisters, and I never knew or cared much about girls 'til I began to teach. Then, I'll own up, I was mightily taken with Amorita, and we got engaged, but she wouldn't let me tell. That ought to have opened my eyes, for there was nothing to be ashamed of, but it didn't. Then Evans Dower came to school, and because he was so taken with you..."

"Oh! Sam, that isn't true, for I hardly know him to speak to," put in Nancy.

"Never mind, Miss Innocence; let me tell my story. Because he was so taken with you, and didn't notice her, Amorita got jealous, and determined to make him like her. Then she began to play fast and loose with me, and to run after him, and I got mad, and we fell out. She broke the engagement, and when I found how glad I was, I knew I had never really loved her. It frightens me when I think how near I came to spoiling my own life, and hers, too."

"I knew about part of it," said Nancy, quietly, "but I thought most of it was very different; and I'm afraid of fellows that don't treat girls as they'd ought to."

"You're right there, Nancy, but I'm not that kind. I've told you the whole truth. I'll own up, I hardly noticed you when you first came to school, I was so taken up with Amorita. And, I confess, to my shame, that I did look down on you; but you worked so hard, and got on so fast, that I couldn't help respecting you. Then I saw all along how good and kind you were to the little children. I saw you helping them with their lessons, many's the time, when I knew you wanted to study your own. And I suppose," added Sam, laughing, "you thought nobody knew how you fed the stray dogs that came into the schoolroom."

Chapter 16: Getting an Education

Nancy glanced up in surprise.

"You forgot that their wagging tails showed over your desk," said he; at which Nancy joined in the laugh.

"Poor things!" she said; "some of 'em are half-starved. They've got feelings, just like us. A heap of dogs are better than them that owns 'em."

"I wish to heaven I'd loved you first, Nancy," Sam said, fervently; "but perhaps I shouldn't have had the sense to appreciate a girl like you if I hadn't had a chance to find out what the other kind was like."

"I'm not so good as you think," spoke up Nancy, quickly. "I'm not always nice to my own folks. I made a big fuss and was sassy to Por 'cause he wouldn't give in to my going to school first-off."

"I don't reckon you made any bigger row than I did at home about the same thing," interrupted Sam, with a grim smile. "I was set on getting an education, too, and my father thought I'd had schooling enough because I had been to school three terms. He wanted me to go to work on the farm for my board and clothes 'til I was twenty-one, and I just wouldn't. That's how I came to leave home. I hated to leave mother, but she thought I was in the right. I'd got to earn money if I was to go to school, so I hired out to Mr. Blackwood, and saved up my wages 'til I had enough to go two winters to Dexter College. I worked for him those two summers, too. Then I took this school, so as to get money enough to go to the Highbridge Academy next year. I'm finding out how little I know, and I've got a lot of hard work before me if I am ever to know enough to amount to anything."

"Oh, Sam, you know such a heap now, and I'm so ignorant, and you'll keep on getting further and further ahead of me. Can't you see I'm not the kind of girl you ought to marry? And I oughtn't to marry, nohow," put in Nancy, as an afterthought.

This recalled Sam to his starting-point. "But you haven't told me yet whether you want to marry me, Nancy. Everything depends on that."

Nancy hung her head in silence.

"Don't you think it is rather hard on me," continued Sam, "for you not even to admit that you like me, after I've told you I loved you and asked you to marry me?"

"Yes, I do like you, Sam," replied Nancy, earnestly.

Sam smiled. He had scored a point.

"But liking isn't loving, little girl. Just say once that you love me."

"I can't say that," Nancy replied, trying to withdraw her hand, as she suddenly became conscious of Sam's tightening grip upon it. He held it fast.

"Can't say what, Nancy?" he asked, demurely.

"I can't say I love you, Sam."

"But you have this moment said it, dear," he interrupted, hastily, "and you surely won't take it back. Don't look so troubled, Nancy; I was only teasing you; but couldn't you try to say it in earnest just once? If you know how my heart aches for your love you'd give me the comfort of hearing you say it was mine, if you cared for me."

Silence again. Then Nancy stirred uneasily, and slipping her hand out of Sam's, put it over her eyes.

"What is it, dear?" he whispered, bending his head to hers.

"I love you, Sam," came softly from her lips, and "God bless you, dear!" from his, as he reverently kissed her golden hair.

After a long silence, Sam said: "You haven't said it quite all yet, Nancy. Do you want to marry me?"

Chapter 16: Getting an Education

"Yes, Sam; I know now I love you, and want to marry you," she replied, meeting his eager eyes fearlessly; and the next moment she was in his arms and his kiss upon her lips.

Her burned arm was still in a sling, but neither of them had spoken of it 'til now, and with quick understanding they both laughed when Sam began to reproach himself for having forgotten it.

"It's dreadful at school without you, Nancy; do hurry up and come back."

"Yes, dear, I will; but don't you allow it's going to be hard for us when they all know?"

"I can stand it if you can, Nancy. I only know I'm lost when you're not there," Sam replied.

"Then I sha'n't care how much fun is poked at us," said Nancy, happily.

When her parents came in from the field, Sam manfully told them his story. They were too much taken by surprise to offer any opposition. In truth, they thought it a very good match for Nancy, whose one concern now was about Sam's people; but he made light of her uneasiness. All the obstacles she had raised on her own side had melted away. She only knew that she felt light-hearted and happy, and sure that everything would turn out all right, since Sam had said so.

When she looked off at the mountains at sunset she thought she had never seen them so lovely. They seemed to quiver in coppery haze before settling into purple shade. Her eyes filled with tears at their inexpressible charm, and beautiful verses from the Psalms floated through her mind.

As the light faded, the world about her fell into shadow; but her own heart was aglow with that divine light which shall never fade from earth 'til time shall be no more.

IV

Nancy's arm was long in healing. By the time she returned to school, her engagement had ceased to be a nine-days' wonder, so things were easier for her and Sam than they had anticipated.

Amorita had left school in disgust when she heard of the engagement, and Evans Dower, finding himself hard hit, left also. He bade Sam good-bye with many good wishes, but frankly owning that he couldn't stand by and see Nancy carried off by another; and Sam thought the more of him for it.

Now that spring was approaching, most of the older pupils had left to work in the fields. A very little extra work on the farm always gave the parents the excuse they wanted to keep the children at home. Anxious to make up for lost time, Nancy plunged eagerly into her school work. The number of pupils being now so small, Sam had plenty of time to help her with her lessons. Her rapid progress was a constant surprise to him. He laughingly told her he believed she'd get ahead of him yet. When alone they discussed their future.

"We can't marry for three years, I'm afraid, dear," said Sam; "and I feel bad to have to keep you waiting so long."

"It won't seem so long," returned Nancy, with a happy smile. "Now I can write, there'll always be your letters to think about, and we've both got a heap of hard work before us, and that will keep us from pining."

"That's true, Nancy. If I am to be a teacher, or get any kind of a situation worth having, I've got a lot to learn, and I mean to do my very best at the Academy this winter. It is hard and slow work getting an education, Nancy. I wonder if it pays."

"Oh, don't say that, Sam, dear! You never talked like that before."

Chapter 16: Getting an Education

"No," laughed Sam; "because I was never really in love before. Now," he added, seriously, "it seems as if nothing that separated you and me is worth having."

"I know," replied Nancy, softly, her eyes filling with tears, "but it's like what the Bible says about putting your hand to the plow and not looking back. I ain't always sure what the kingdom of God means, but I reckon love and doing what's right is part of it."

As the time of the separation so dreaded by them both drew near, they walked together in the woods, feigning an interest in Nature's ever-new miracles, but their thoughts were upon other things. While the new galax leaves were shooting everywhere underfoot, they noted the old ones growing sere and the flower-stalks rising in soldierly array among them. "They'll soon be in blossom, Sam," Nancy would begin, brightly, but she would end with a quick sob as she suddenly remembered that when that time came he would be far away.

"Look down into the coves, Nancy," said Sam; "you can see the spring beginning to creep up the mountains."

"No, no, I don't want to see it; when it gets to the top you'll be gone," and Nancy hid her face against his shoulder. Sam kissed the bowed head, and they went on in silence.

When Sam turned the key for the last time in the schoolhouse door, Nancy found courage to tell the story of the offerings she had placed upon his desk.

"And you didn't really care for me all that time, Nancy? After I found out it wasn't Amorita, I was fool enough to think it was some other girl who was in love with me, but I never thought of you. Afterward I got so interested in you that I forgot all about it."

"No, Sam, I didn't care for you; I was only sorry for you because you seemed so unhappy."

"Well, Nancy, I'm glad it was you who befriended me those hard days – for they were hard, I can tell you."

Sam was to leave on the morrow, and Nancy had cried herself to sleep. Long before day she awoke with sudden pang of loss, and youth's intolerance of misery. Except for the gleam of smoldering coals in the fireplace, the homely room was in darkness, and the rest of the family were asleep. Nancy rose, and dressing herself quietly, threw a shawl over her head and slipped out of doors. Nip, the hound, came running to meet her, and followed her to the spring, glad to have the long night-watch shared by another.

As she bent over the stream and dashed the cold water into her face, her hands clung to her eyes, and she began to sob afresh.

Nip pawed imperatively at her arm, but she took no notice 'til he began to whine. "Don't do that, good old nip; we mustn't wake up the rest," she said, patting him; and he lay down, reassured. Nancy leaned against the old maple-tree that overhung the spring, staying her sobs for the sake of keeping the dog quiet, but talking softly to herself the while. "Oh, why did I let him go? He would have staid if I had said the word. He's right; nothing is worth while that parts us. It was easy enough to be brave for both of us so long as I had him. I didn't know it could be like this," she murmured, brokenly. "If I had – well, if I had, I'd have done just the same, for I knew it was the right thing. I mustn't let Sam know what a coward I've been," she said, beginning to walk restlessly to and fro. It was good to be out in the frosty air under the stars, but she could not remain long in one place. She listened mechanically to the creaking of dead limbs on the trees, and she heard the sharp bark of a fox in the distance and the nearer jangle of cow-bells, but none of these noises seemed to belong to her world any more.

Suddenly a sound as of one in distress set her senses at attention. As she stopped short to listen, Nip bounded past her to the seat under the big spruce pine, and Nancy caught the words, "Good old Nip! Is that you?" softly spoken. She sprang toward the voice, and the next instant her arms were about Sam's neck, and they were

Chapter 16: Getting an Education

weeping together as if the lights of heaven had been eternally extinguished for them.

Nancy, in whom the first flush of grief was well-nigh spent, was the first to regain self-control.

"Don't Sam, darling; I didn't know a man could cry so," she said.

"Nor I either 'til now, Nancy," he replied, with an attempt to laugh.

"I can't go, dear," he said, presently.

Nancy caught her breath. Was not this the answering note to her heart-cry, "I can't let him go!" which had rung through her brain for hours at a time? What should she do? Sam was older, and knew so much more than she did; perhaps, after all, he was right, and nothing which parted them was worth while. Life was so short and so uncertain! What could she do against fate? And this seemed like the hand of fate turning them back.

All this and much more swept through her mind while she grew outwardly calm and tried to comfort Sam by silent caresses. Then she spoke: "I'm only a girl, Sam, and I'm awfully ignorant, but I've had some hard things to go through. I never seem to know what's right at the time, and I get all mixed up. Then I try to think how I sensed it before I was in the thick of it, and to go by that. I reckon that's what we've got to do now. it was like death when I got awake this morning, and I had to come out of doors to get my breath; but I know we are in the right, and we must hold fast to that, no matter what comes. If you stayed now because of me, it would mean that I had spoiled your life, for there's nothing here for a man like you to do."

Sam, still sobbing at intervals, said nothing, and she continued, "I didn't mean you ever to know how I'd broke down."

"Nor I you, Nancy," he interrupted, "but the mischief's done now."

"It's no mischief, Sam," Nancy replied, more cheerfully. "It's done us both a sight of good; and while you are away I shall never love you better than when I think how we cried here together. But you must go now, dear, or you'll miss the train at the Junction."

For an instant Sam's sobs mastered him. Nancy clung to him, but her own eyes were dry. Then he strained her to his breast, kissing her eyes and lips.

"It needn't be good-bye quite yet, Nancy. Come with me as far as Eagle's Crag, and wave to me across the gorge. It will be sun-up by the time I get round to the Knob," he said.

When Sam was gone, Nancy, sitting on the mossy rocks, waiting for sunrise, swayed back and forth with her head bowed upon her knees. Nip thrust his nose under her arm, but she pushed him away. She could not yet tolerate a living touch in this chaos of misery that enveloped her. The tide of sorrow which she hoped had ebbed for good had turned, and only the feeling that it would be like disloyalty to Sam to give way again kept her from crying aloud.

From one of the coves at the foot of the gorge there came up the cry of a child. It touched her strangely. "Is there a wave of misery spreading over the whole earth?" she thought, "and was the child's cry a part of it? God help us all!" she exclaimed, as she felt herself one of this brotherhood of sorrow.

When the sun rayed on the eastern horizon, the coldness of the night melted suddenly into the soft balminess of the new spring. The mountain-peaks stand forth in silver armor, sending up welcoming tongues of mist as the sun touches their snowy summits.

Nancy stood upon Eagle's Crag, and as she did so Sam stepped forth into the sunshine upon a similar boulder on the other side of the great chasm which now divided them. From the depths below, smoke was struggling above the trees from unseen chimneys, and the sounds of a new day awoke the echoes. Here a belated ax rang upon the wood for the morning fire; there the bleat of a stray sheep mingled with the lowing of cattle, the crowing of cocks, and the barking of dogs. Nor were human notes wanting. But these two, standing above it all, were blind and deaf to everything but their own misery.

With a show of bravery they answered one another's signals, and Nancy stood firm 'til Sam went on his way and a turn in the road hid him from her sight. Then a black mist seemed suddenly to drop between her and the world. The next two hours were a blank to her. At the end of that time she went wearily home. Her mother, who a moment before had stood in the doorway looking anxiously up and down the road, met her with cheerful unconcern.

"I thought you'd be along right soon," she said. "I sot the coffee and the pone nigh the fire to keep hot for you. Better bile yourself a new-laid egg. The children's gone to Aunt Maria's to spend the day. She's been pesterin' me to let 'em come. Por, he's gone to help Mr. Burns plow, and he done took his snack along with him. I 'lowed you and me could do all as wants doing at home."

Nancy kissed her mother, without a word.

V

"I was so heartsick over leaving you," Sam's first letter to Nancy ran, "that I thought every moment I must turn back; but when I saw you on Eagle's Crag you seemed like my good angel, encouraging me to go forward, and I plucked up heart again."

Later he wrote: "I shall accomplish more this year than I thought I could. I got more education out of teaching last winter than I realized, and now everything comes that much easier. I'm away ahead of a lot of the fellows already. Nobody here knows about my little Nancy. I keep her picture locked up in my trunk, but she never misses a good-night kiss, I can tell you."

Nancy, in her turn, wrote: "You do write such a fine hand, and such a beautiful letter, dearest Sam, that I'm ashamed of mine. It's good of you to like them, though. I'm trying hard to write better, and I study the lessons you marked out for me every chance I get."

During the first year of their separation Nancy attended every school session within her reach. At the end of that time she was given a certificate which entitled her to apply for a position as teacher of one of the county free schools. This placed her upon the same footing as that held by Sam when he took the Wren Hill school. It made her a proud and happy girl, but, like Sam, she had discovered that her feet were only upon the lowest rounds of the ladder of knowledge.

At this time she had what she regarded as a great stroke of luck. She was offered a scholarship in one of the best of the mountain mission schools.

"Isn't it almost too good to believe?" she wrote Sam. "It isn't only what I shall learn from books I think of. There's cooking and sewing and all kinds of useful things taught there. The best of it is, the teachers are real ladies, and I shall learn more lessons from them than they know of. I am so anxious to be worthy of you, dear Sam. You shall have no cause to be ashamed of me, if I can help it. I thought Pa would oppose my leaving home for so many months, but he is so taken up with some plans of his own, just now that he don't seem to care. I'll tell you about that another time."

Nancy spent the better part of the next two years at this school, while Sam, after graduating from the Academy, got a position as bookkeeper in a town in the eastern part of the state. It was too far away to permit of his return home during his brief holidays, so he and Nancy did not meet during three years. If it sometimes crossed his mind, amid his new surroundings, that he had probably made a mistake in choosing for his wife a girl like Nancy, he did not harbor the thought. Despite these occasional misgivings, he remained loyal to her, determined in the depths of his heart to make her happy and

Chapter 16: Getting an Education

to accept manfully for himself whatever of the worse, as well as the better, of marriage should befall them.

He had seen no one from home, and since the death of his mother, in the first year of his absence, he rarely received a letter, except from Nancy, so his only knowledge of the home happenings came through her.

She had sent him no new photograph of herself, although he had begged for one. So he thought of the girl he loved as looking just as she did when he bade her good-bye, and in his mind's eye he always saw her amid the same humble surroundings.

When the time came to write and ask her to name an early day for their marriage, Nancy's reply was a surprise to him. After telling him how glad she was that their long waiting was at an end, she added: "I've never told you that I was not the only one of my people getting an education. I thought it better to wait and see how things turned out; but now that the time of our reunion is at hand, my heart misgives me lest you think I haven't been frank with you, dear Sam. That's why I am spoiling the fine surprise I had for you by telling you the story now.

After I began to read papers and books to Pa and Ma, they looked at some things in a new light, and wanted to live better. It did me good to see the change, and I was often on the point of speaking of it in my letters. Afterward I wanted to surprise you.

There was no good reason for our living as we did, for Pa had money laid by; but he was always saying that what had been good enough for his father was good enough for him. The year you left, some of the summer boarders offered him a good price for the ridge land, where the view is so fine; so he sold it, and they put up three pretty cottages there. All that building going on put Pa in the notion of building a new house himself. When he makes up his mind to do a thing there's no stopping him, you know; so the house was soon finished. And what is more, it is comfortably furnished, even to a good organ. I've learned to play and sing quite respectably. That was another surprise I had for you. After the new house was done, Pa said he wanted the family to dress better, and that had made a great difference in their appearance. The children go to school regularly, so you see we are all, old and young, getting an education. I'm the only thing about the old place, dear Sam, that isn't much changed." That was all she said about herself.

When Sam went home to claim his bride, he was met at the door of her father's smart new house by a young lady with a gently gravity of manner, who invited him into the best room. He was sure he had seen her before, but where? While trying to remember, he asked, "Is Miss Nancy Rivers at home?" "Yes," she replied, sedately, and left the room.

She returned in a moment with a radiant face and outstretched hands, which, in some confusion, he took in his own. Then as the light fell full upon her laughing face, it was revealed to him where he had seen her before.

"My God, Nancy, what a lovely girl you've grown to be!" he cried, drawing her into his arms and kissing her; "and to think I didn't know you, darling."

"That's the best of it, Sam. I was so afraid I wasn't really improved, and that folks who said I was were flatterers. I wanted so to be worthy of you, dear. And oh, Sam! how handsome you are yourself! I'm so proud of you!"

"Proud of me, indeed, Nancy! Why, I'm nothing beside you. How have you done it all?"

"I suppose it is all part of getting an education," replied Nancy, soberly. "It brings the tears to my eyes sometimes when I think how my determination to get an education has educated my whole family, too. You needn't be ashamed of any of us now, Sam."

"Great heavens, child, I'm so proud of you that my head is quite turned! Now that I have a good look at you, Nancy, I don't know how I dared to kiss you when you came in."

Chapter 16: Getting an Education

"Nonsense, Sam," Nancy replied, lightly kissing his cheek. "You see I'm not afraid of kissing you."

"I should hope not, dear," returned Sam; "but you've been just my little Nancy to me all these years. Now you're grown into such a" – Nancy playfully put her hand over his mouth. He kissed her hand and took it in his own. "Yes, let me say it, Nancy. You've grown into such a beautiful young woman that I feel all at sea."

"But you love me just the same?" Nancy asked, in a troubled voice.

Sam's reply satisfied her.

Presently he took a tiny box from his vest-pocket, saying: "See, Nancy, here's your wedding ring. Try if it will fit you." She slipped it on. "Yes," he said, raising her hand to his lips and kissing the ring. "My blessing on it, and you, my darling," he whispered.

"How like your dear old self!" said Nancy, laying her head on his shoulder. "Don't be foolish about me any more, Sam. You made me feel quite strange at first."

"Did I? Well, I felt quite strange myself," he replied, with a happy laugh.

"And I am really to put that ring on your finger for good day after to-morrow?" he added, seriously. "It's all like a beautiful dream coming true."

Like Other Children

It was not to be expected that a mountain town with a boom in the offing should take thought for free schools. Such at least was the opinion held by the authorities of Redbank. That was twenty years ago. If poor people would persist in being drawn into the town by interest or curiosity, their swarming hordes of children must take their chances.

The talk was all of how everything would "float" when the boom struck. Small heed fell to the share of a floating population, a large contingent of which belonged to the great unwashed.

Fortunately, there were benevolent strangers also within the gates. As a drop in the bucket of educational need, some of these started a sewing-school for girls. Among the pupils was a little girl named Rosie Blake. She was a quaint little figure in her dark stiff gown reaching to her heels. Her faded light hair, strained back from a high, narrow forehead, was braided into a long, thin pigtail, tied at the end with a white string. She might have stepped out of one of those queer sketches of Porte Crayon's of ante-bellum days.

Her gentle ways, and a quick, responsive smile that relieved her angular face from plainness, made her a very attractive little person in the school. It was called a sewing-school, but lessons in manners and household duties played a very important part in its work.

Rosie proved so apt a pupil that she was much missed when she suddenly disappeared from the school. None of the other children knew anything about her, except where she lived. This was so far out of town that it was nearly a month before Miss Dollard, one of the teachers, could spare the time to visit her. She found Rosie's family living in a new cabin, built in the woods, on as primitive principles as though no growing town were near at hand.

"I allowed when I see you comin' that you was one o' the teachers Rosie set sich store by in sewin'-school," said Mrs. Blake, coming forward to shake hands. "Have a chair."

Rosie placed a chair for Miss Dollard. Then with a bob of her head and a duck of her lank figure intended for a curtsy, she withdrew behind her mother.

Mrs. Blake, viewing Rosie's fine manners with pride, exclaimed: "You-uns done learned Rosie a sight! I were plum sorry she had to quit school."

"I hope she hasn't left for good," replied Miss Dollard. "That's what I came to see you about."

"'Bleeged to you, I'm sure," Mrs. Blake rejoined; "but I don't guess you-all heard what a sight o' trouble we-uns been havin'?"

"No," answered Miss Dollard; "we have heard nothing since Rosie left school."

"I can't rightly talk about it yet," said Mrs. Blake, with a choke in her voice. "We-uns buried our Nancy last week--our gal next older nor Rosie. She had pneumony fever. She were sick nigh on to a month. her and the older gals worked in the mill. Rosie and two o' the least ones has been right bad off, too. Rosie took sick tendin' on Nancy, and she ain't been right peart since."

While expressing her sympathy, Miss Dollard looked kindly at the little group gathered about the mother. Besides a baby in arms there were two younger than Rosie.

Following her glance, Mrs. Blake said: "This ain't all. Sammy's done hid; he's ashamed."

"Ashamed?" said Miss Dollard.

"His face is queer," she explained. "He were born that way. Folks laughs at him, and looks at him so sharp 'pears like he can't stand it, nohow. He's a right peart little chap, and the lovingest you ever see. I didn't reckon he'd be afraid of you, 'count o' the way

Chapter 17: Like Other Children

Rosie's always talkin' about you, but I don't guess he knowed who you was. He mostly hides when he sees anybody comin'. Mirandy and Rushy's away at the mill. We-uns is powerful lonesome without Nancy," added she, wiping her eyes on her apron; "she were the peartest of 'em all."

Rosie was quietly crying into a little handkerchief, which Miss Dollard recognized as a product of the sewing-school. The other children sniveling sympathetically, appealing at intervals to Rosie for the loan of her handkerchief, which was evidently a great novelty to them all.

"I don't guess you knowed Miss Dayton from Ohio, did you?" inquired Mrs. Blake, presently.

"Say you didn't? Well, she stopped at the Hill House all winter, and she were mighty good to we-uns. She come every Sunday evening and had Sunday-school. She most learned them least ones to spell and read. She's done gone away now," Mrs. Blake added, with a sigh. "First we-uns see of her she come every Sunday evenin' to read the Bible to Aunt Dinah, a pore old nigger that lives in yon house," she continued, pointing to a wretched cabin in the pines near by.

"The children set a heap o' store by Aunt Dinah, and they kept a-runnin' in and out when Miss Dayton were there. They sot by when she were readin', and she were right friendly with 'em. Sometimes she brung 'em candy. The children liked her splendid. After a bit she came in to see me. She said weren't we-uns goin' to give the children no schoolin', and why didn't they go to Sunday-school. I done told her the plain truth; we-uns was too poor to send 'em. She allowed as they might go to Sunday-school, and talked somethin' out o' the Bible about without money and without price.

I up and told her how Nancy and Rosie here done tried it, and the rich folks' children laughed at their poor clothes and plain ways. When they was comin' along home, some on 'em hollered out to t'others to look at some o' father Noah's family, and axed 'em did they just come out o' the ark. Nancy and Rosie felt might mean 'count o' havin' fun poked at 'em, but they didn't know who Noah was then. That were before Miss Dayton read 'em Bible stories. That's how Rosie come to go to sewing-school. She allowed as you-uns would learn her manners, so she needn't be shy of folks. She done learned a sight, ain't you, Rosie?"

"Yes, marm," replied Rosie, smiling through her tears at Miss Dollard.

"Arter a bit," Mrs. Blake resumed, "Miss Dayton said did we-uns want a sunday-school every Sunday evenin'. I done told her yes, and be thankful. That's how she got to comin'. She done learned the children a sight out o' the Bible, and Nancy were that peart she could tell a heap of it over to her Pa afterwards. When she took sick Miss Dayton come to see her, and set with her. She talked mighty pretty and consolin' to her and we-uns when Nancy were a-dyin'. It were a sight o' comfort," said the mother, with a heavy sigh.

"Miss Dayton allowed as Nancy were one o' the Lord's little ones the Bible talks about, and we needn't be afraid He wouldn't take care of her. Nancy died smilin' up into her face, listenin' to her pretty talk," Mrs. Blake added, crying quietly into her apron. After a pause, she said: "Rosie knows a right smart o' stories Miss Dayton read out o' the Bible, don't you, Rosie?" Rosie's cheeks flushed deeply, but she made no reply. Her mother, taking no notice of her, went on: "Last night, when we all was in bed, and the fire burnin' low, so the room were all shadows, she were tellin' such a pretty one. It were about Mary and Marthy. Tell it to the lady, Rosie," said her mother in a tone of authority.

Miss Dollard, who had been looking at the three beds the room contained, and wondering if the whole family slept in such close quarters, glanced kindly at poor Rosie, who had turned pale at her mother's abrupt request.

"Do, Rosie; I should so like to hear it," she said, taking the child's hand in hers.

The lessons in manners which Rosie had so valued at sewing-school came to her aid. Swallowing hard, she began, in a shaky voice: "Onct there was two sisters. Their names was Mary and Marthy. They was friends of the Lord, and He were comin' to see 'em. Marthy heard it when she were doin' a errand at one o' the neighbors. She run home right quick, and done told Mary, and axed her would she help her slick the house up a bit before he come. But Mary wouldn't. She just sot round, sayin' how pleased she were, but Marthy went hoppin' about pickin' the crumbs off the floor," said Rosie, bringing her story to an abrupt termination.

Her mother nodded smilingly at Miss Dollard to express her admiration for Rosie's gifts as a story-teller, while Miss Dollard, patting the child's hand and thanking her, rose to go.

Before leaving she asked Mrs. Blake if they would like their Sunday-school continued, if one of the other teachers and herself could take charge of it. The offer was gratefully accepted, and for many months Miss Dollard and Miss Nelson devoted their Sunday afternoons to the Blakes. The young people from a household close by were regular attendants, so that the Sunday-school often numbered fifteen or twenty pupils, varying in age from the baby up to young women of twenty-five.

Miss Dayton's plan of following the usual Sunday-school work with a lesson in reading and writing was continued. The elder pupils, who had never been to school, learned with difficulty, but the eagerness of the younger ones to master the three R's gave zest to the work. Tommy, the baby, sat on the bare floor, finding endless amusement in poking crumbs of green soda biscuit through the gaping cracks. He laughed with glee when the chickens under the house noisily squabbled for them. If a greedy one nabbed his finger, Sunday-school took a recess 'til he was pacified.

Poor little Sammy, with his disfigured face and dreadful stutter, was the brightest of all the pupils. It was painful to look at him, but he soon won the affections of his teachers, who decided that something must be done to prevent his going through life bearing so disfiguring a birth-mark. After learning that he could be successfully operated upon at the new hospital near Redbank, Miss Dollard broached the subject to his mother.

To her consternation, Mrs. Blake exclaimed: "No, sir! The Lord *made* him that way, and we-uns ain't goin' agin' the Lord! If He'd a' meant Sammy to be like other children, why didn't He make him so in the first place? Besides, supposin' he should die? Me and his Pa wouldn't never forgive ourselves for givin' in to what you-uns is talkin' about."

Arguments and pleadings were of no avail. The more the teachers saw of the child, however, the more determined they were to save his sensitive spirit future suffering. They had seen little of the father, but were told that he was even "more sot agin' a operation" than the mother. Sunday after Sunday they returned to the charge, but were constantly met by the humiliation of defeat.

Sammy listened with eager interest whenever the subject was broached. The teachers had at first feared his opposition, but they little knew what pluck he had.

One Sunday Mrs. Blake said, reproachfully: "Sammy says if his Pa and me won't let him get his face fixed, he's bound to run off to the hospital and beg the doctors to do it right quick, before we-uns knows where he's at."

To her surprise and disgust, Miss Dollard laughed. Then turning to Sammy she said: "That's right, my boy. It is you who will have to suffer all your life if it isn't done, and your parents will be glad by and by that you had your way in this."

Although the father and mother still withheld their consent, the teachers felt from that hour that the victory was won. When the parents finally yielded, Miss Dollard hurried the child to the hospital, where the operation was performed almost immediately.

Chapter 17: Like Other Children

The mother was permitted to act as nurse during Sammy's convalescence. "Ain't it just wonderful how easy-like the doctors done it?" she said, when the teachers visited the patient. "I ain't never had no use for doctors and doctors' stuff before, but I ain't a-goin' agin' 'em no more. Just to think that Sammy'll look like other children now, and needn't hide hisself for shame no more! And it's all along o' you-uns. I used to have hard feelin's agin' you, 'count o' your not givin' in about Sammy, but I can't tell you how thankful I be to you now. I sha'n't never forget what you-uns and the doctors done for Sammy."

They were sitting beside the child's cot, full of thankfulness and relief themselves that all was well. The poor little face was so enveloped in bandages that only the eager eyes could speak, but at his mother's words Sammy stretched out his hands to his teachers, who clasped them in their own. The mother, quick to interpret the child's gestures, said: "He's a-tryin' to thank you-uns the best he knows how, now he can't talk."

Dear little man! How patiently he had borne, and was still bearing, all the pain and discomfort.

To be like other children had been the haunting desire of his life. He had been as one in bondage, and now he was free. By many little arts and dumb gestures he made his teachers understand that he felt that it was to them, first of all, that he owed his freedom. As soon as he could talk, he said to them: "Now I can go to free school when it starts, and not be ashamed no more. If it hadn't been for you-uns I wouldn't never have looked like other children."

The mother was fairly crying for joy.

"I can't never thank you-uns enough for not givin' in to my contrariness about Sammy," she said. "I hated it that bad to see him like that I'd a' given my right hand to cure him. Folks allowed as it were goin' agin' the Lord to meddle with such things, though, and we-uns reckoned he'd die if we give in to have the operation. 'Peared like we just couldn't stand it."

Not long after Sammy's recovery, Miss Dollard and Miss Nelson were obliged to leave Redbank.

The opening of free schools about that time, however, gave the Blakes and other poor children a coveted chance for "eddication." There was also started near the Blakes a mission Sunday-school, which the poorest and humblest might attend, unabashed by their lack of fine raiment.

About the Author

Mary Nelson Carter was not always a "southern writer" as advertised by her original publisher. She was a Northerner from a family of New England Yankees. The daughter of a well-heeled merchant captain from Nantucket and an Irish mother, the family lived in New York City, and later Fairfield, Connecticut. Their historic pre-Revolution home is one of the few buildings in Fairfield to survive the war, and is still standing today.

In 1863 she married a New Yorker, Charles Carter, at All Saint's Church, in New York City. He had served as a doctor in the union army, and they were married while the Civil war still raged. After the war they relocated to the Philadelphia area where Charles began a medical practice. It was from there that their life-long love of the mountains of North Carolina began. After making several extended trips to that area, they fell in love with the people and the culture of the mountains around Blowing Rock. Finally, due to an epidemic that hit the area in the 1880s they decided that his skills as a physician were needed by the folks of Blowing Rock, more than by the people of Philadelphia, so, Blowing Rock became their new home. Mary died there in 1908, ten years after her husband.

Mary Carter and her husband are both remembered in Blowing Rock for their contributions to the community. In Mary's case it was her long work fighting illiteracy in the region, and the establishment of a free library, in a building they built right on the lawn beside their house, that secured her place in the town's history. Her "Lend-A-Hand Library" which she started, working with Reverend William Savage, the Episcopal minister in Blowing Rock, slowly grew over the years, until, in 1928, long after her death, it became the Blowing Rock Community and School Library. Her only known work to date,

North Carolina Sketches: Phases of Life Where the Galax Grows was published in 1900. It was originally released a part of a three-part series of books about local cultures of the south. It will be joined, later in 2012, by a previously unknown work, begun by her, but not completed before her death.

Contact Information

INFONOUVEAU
P.O. BOX 10542
ROCHESTER, NY. 14610
EMAIL: INFO@INFONOUVEAU.COM

Capital Short Stories of the South
By Clever Southern Writers

Typical Mountain Scenery in the South.

Tennessee Sketches. *By* Louise Preston Looney
North Carolina Sketches. *By* Mary Nelson Carter
Northern Georgia Sketches. *By* Will N. Harben

Three volumes, 16mo, neatly bound.

THE sketches contained in these volumes seem to be written by the people who are written about. The characteristics and the dialect of the section are treated in natural and convincing fashion, and the stories are all full of human interest. They are indeed exceptionally entertaining contributions to the knowledge of local traits.

The visitor or sojourner in the South will find the humor of these sketches contagious. They will quicken the enjoyment of the quaint and curious customs of the people of the mountain and of the valley.

Price of each volume, $1.00

PLEASE ORDER OF YOUR BOOKSELLER, OR
IF NO BOOKSTORE IS CONVENIENT YOUR POSTMASTER WILL ORDER FOR YOU

A. C. McClurg & Co., Publishers, Chicago

Proof

Made in the USA
Charleston, SC
06 July 2012